# The Jerome Conspiracy
## Third Edition

*Michael Wood*

Tubi Publishing, LLC

# Acknowledgments

To Osvaldo Jerez and Esteban Serrano who have laboriously critiqued more than three dozen versions of this manuscript word for word.

To David Compton who meticulously styled my words into much better prose.

# Chapter One

1952—Vatican City, Rome

"Enter," the cardinal commanded, responding to a knock on his office door.

An elderly bishop walked in, knelt down, and kissed the cardinal's ring before he began to speak. "You told me to inform you if any of the scrolls we discovered could be of concern to the Church."

"Yes?" the cardinal responded, rapidly drumming his fingers on the desk.

The bishop gulped. "I'm troubled about some of the scrolls found in cave number four."

The cardinal leaned forward.

The bishop's voice started shaking. "These scrolls reveal something quite disturbing." He handed the cardinal a written summary of his discovery.

The cardinal read the report and grimaced. "Have you shared your findings with anyone else?"

"No, Your Grace … I wanted you to be the first to know, just as you ordered."

The cardinal leaned back. "If these scrolls are made public, someone else might put the same pieces together. And we cannot allow that to happen. You must never discuss your findings with anyone, even other members of the cloth. Simply tell the others that I have ordered for all the scrolls found in cave four to be kept secret indefinitely. And leave it at that. Do you understand?"

"Yes, Your Grace," the bishop replied. Then he promptly turned around and exited the room.

# Chapter Two

Present Day—San Francisco, California

"Turn left at the next light," Peter told Jamie. "Let's take the highway home."

Jamie glanced at the clock on the dashboard. "I can't believe its three o'clock in the morning. We haven't been out this late in ages."

"The music was amazing."

"Yeah," Jamie said with a smile as he turned to look at Peter. "And the—"

¤ ¤ ¤

Peter opened his eyes. Everything looked fuzzy. It took a moment for his eyes to focus, and when they did he saw a young nurse standing next to him. "What happened?"

"You've been in a very bad car accident," the woman replied. "Try to get some rest now."

Peter's mind rushed to Jamie. "Jamie! Where's Jamie?"

"The doctor will be here shortly. He'll tell you everything. Just try to relax."

"I need to see Jamie," Peter insisted. "Where is he?"

A frown crossed the nurse's face. "Let me see what I can do."

¤ ¤ ¤

At three-thirty in the morning, everything was quiet in the Webber household. Samantha, a middle-aged housewife, was sleeping comfortably next to her husband, Jonathon. Beside the bed lay a worn

Bible that Samantha and Jonathon—a devout evangelical Christian couple—often read together before retiring to sleep.

Acceptance of the Bible as God's inerrant, literal truth was the foundation of the couple's life. Every week they faithfully attended four church services: Sunday school, Sunday morning service, Sunday evening service, and Wednesday night prayer. And once every quarter, they attended seven straight days of evening revival services. When they listened to the radio, they often tuned to a Christian station. And their reading material was also generally limited to Christian topics presented from an evangelical perspective.

Samantha and Jonathon were both awakened by the ringing telephone. "Who in the world would call us at this time of the night?" Samantha wondered as her husband answered the phone.

When she saw the color drain from her husband's face, Samantha felt a tight knot in the pit of her stomach. "What is it? Is it Jamie?"

Jonathon choked on his words as he spoke into the phone. "I appreciate you calling us so quickly. We'll be there as soon as we can."

Jonathon hung up.

Samantha stared at her husband, waiting for him to respond.

As tears welled up in Jonathon's eyes, he reached for his wife's hand. "That was Holy Cross Hospital. Jamie's been in a bad accident, and the doctor doesn't believe he has much time left. We need to take the next flight to San Francisco."

At that moment, Samantha envisioned Jamie's soul writhing in a sweltering lake of fire. And she heard him uttering blood curdling shrieks as the flames persistently burned his soul from every direction.

Samantha was terror stricken at the thought of her only child spending eternity imprisoned in the fires of hell. She stopped breathing for a moment. But then a sudden surge of strength and determination overcame her. One thought began to consume her mind: she *must* make sure her son would be saved from that horrible fate.

Getting dressed, making reservations, driving to the airport, waiting for the flight—it was all one big blur. On the plane, Samantha began to reminisce over the miraculous way Jamie had entered the world.

The Webbers had been trying to get pregnant for more than three years. One day after church, they made a comment to their pastor about their frustrating attempts. That week, during Wednesday night prayer, Pastor Rick had asked them to stand before the congregation. After the pastor explained their problem, the members of the church came forward and laid their hands on the couple as they compassionately prayed to God on their behalf.

Samantha remembered how, two months after that, she realized she hadn't had her regular period. Secretly—not wanting to get Jonathon's hopes up—she went for a pregnancy test. It was a miracle: the result came back positive. The Webbers had always considered Jamie their priceless gift from God.

But there were other memories of Jamie, some not as pleasant. Samantha couldn't help recalling what had been, until now, the worst day of her life.

One summer afternoon, when Jamie was home during college break, Samantha entered his room to ask him if he had something to tell her about his relationship with David, a neighborhood guy about Jamie's own age. Jamie looked startled, then afraid. Samantha assured him she would always love him no matter what. And that was when— after much squirming and shifting in his chair—Jamie blurted out those horrible words: "Mom, I'm gay." When Samantha heard those words, she became physically sick to her stomach.

Samantha was jolted from her recollection when a flight attendant announced it was time to prepare for landing. She held firmly to her resolve. "Jonathon, we need to ask Jamie if he's accepted Jesus as his personal savior the moment we arrive. I can't even imagine how I could survive if our only child ends up spending eternity in hell."

The frown on Jonathon's face deepened. "Honey, in all the confusion I forgot to tell you Jamie's unconscious. The doctor doesn't think he'll regain consciousness. Whatever you have to say to him, we'll just have to hope he'll hear it on some level."

Samantha wrapped her arms defiantly around herself. "No. I can't accept this. Jonathon, how did the doctor know to call our house?

Was Jamie conscious when he arrived at the hospital?"

Jonathon squeezed his wife's hand. "No, sweetheart. Jamie had a medical alert card in his wallet. He listed you as the person to contact in a medical emergency."

Samantha's shoulders began to sag, and she hung her head. She began to pray. "God, wake my baby up when I'm there. *I trust you with the salvation of my son's soul.*"

An incredible wave of peace came over her. In her heart of hearts, she knew she was going to see her boy on the other side.

¤ ¤ ¤

When Samantha and Jonathon arrived at the hospital, the attendant informed them that only one visitor was permitted in the intensive care unit at a time.

Jonathon gently placed his hand on his wife's shoulder. "You go first."

Jamie was still unconscious when Samantha arrived. There were machines attached to him from head to toe. She brushed back the light brown hair from his forehead to give him a kiss. "Jamie," she whispered into his ear. "It's me. Mom."

Samantha could swear her son's eyelids flickered. "Honey, if you can hear me, I need you to show me somehow that you have accepted Jesus. Jamie, please let me know somehow that you have accepted Jesus."

Jamie opened his eyes.

Goosebumps danced on Samantha's arms. She was sure this was the answer to her prayers.

"Mom," Jamie said weakly.

Samantha pressed. "Honey, I'm so afraid time may be running out. Please let me know. Have you accepted Jesus?"

Jamie smiled. "No, Mom. I don't believe in all that religious stuff. I've never believed in it. You know that."

"Honey, I'm begging you," she pleaded. "Surrender to God right now. I can't bear the thought of your soul suffering forever in hell. Please, Jamie, this is serious."

Jamie's words faltered, but he remained calm and relaxed. "Mom … if God exists, I'm sure he must be the way Peter says. He'd have to be the most loving, wonderful being. Mom … I'm not afraid."

And with that, Jamie closed his eyes.

Samantha gripped the bedrails tightly. "Jamie, now isn't the time to be stubborn. The reality is that the eternal fate of your soul depends on what—" She was interrupted by loud beeps from the machines attached to her son's body.

# Chapter Three

Within seconds the head nurse rushed into the room. "Mrs. Webber, please go to the waiting area."

Samantha didn't budge. "No. I'm staying here with Jamie."

The nurse glared at her. "Mrs. Webber, you must let us tend to him!"

Samantha stood and moved about three feet from the bed. "I'll step out of the way, but I'm not leaving my boy."

The nurse walked toward her. "Mrs. Webber, I didn't want to be the one to tell you, but Jamie's gone."

In shock, Samantha stammered, "No, that isn't possible. God hasn't saved him yet. Jamie can't be …" Samantha became too numb to speak. Her only child had died without accepting Jesus into his heart. She was now certain she would never see her boy in heaven. And even worse, she knew his soul was going to be cast into the everlasting lake of fire when Jesus returned to the earth. The death, the damnation. It was too much for an evangelical Christian mother to bear.

Samantha broke down and cried.

¤ ¤ ¤

When Samantha entered the intensive care unit, Jonathon made his way to the visitor's waiting area. A distinguished-looking gentleman seated next to him noticed the troubled look on his face.

"Are you okay?" the man asked.

"My son Jamie was in a car accident," Jonathon said. "The doctor doesn't think my boy has much time left. And I'm so afraid that he hasn't committed his life to Christ, and it's his roommate's fault. Peter's convinced my son that everyone will eventually go to heaven.

He's convinced Jamie there is no hell."

"So Peter believes the same thing that the original Christians believed," the stranger said nonchalantly.

Jonathon thought he must have misunderstood the stranger's comment. "I'm sorry, what did you say?"

"I'm a history professor at SU. I often lecture on religious history. One of the things I teach my students is that the first Christians believed every human soul will eventually be reconciled to God. The original Christians taught that when Jesus returns, the souls of unbelievers will be temporarily sent to a place called Gehenna for purification while believers get to enjoy a special reward for having lived righteously."

Jonathon was incredulous. "So that's what you teach at your secular institution? I can't imagine how many of your students will lose their eternal souls because of the deceitful lies you teach at your college."

"I don't make judgment calls about theological matters in my lectures. I just teach history," the professor responded matter-of-factly. "Personally, I don't have any religious beliefs—Christian or otherwise. And I'm concerned that your beliefs will cause you a lot of unnecessary suffering if things don't work out the way you want with your son."

The professor reached into his pocket, pulled out a business card, and placed it in Jonathon's hand. "I hope everything works out for you and your family. But if you need someone to talk to, feel free to give me a call."

Jonathon was indignant. He knew the professor's humanistic teachings were responsible for damning legions of souls to hell. He was just about to shove the card back into the professor's hand when he saw Samantha stumbling toward him, looking dazed. Without saying another word, he leaped from his chair, instinctively put the card in his pocket, and rushed toward her.

"Can I go see Jamie now?" Jonathon asked. But when Samantha started sobbing, he knew his son was gone. "Honey, did you get a chance to talk to him?" Jonathon could barely choke out the words.

Samantha nodded, sobbing too hard to speak.

"Did Jamie ask Jesus to come into his heart?"

nightmare."

The pastor touched Jonathon's arm. "I know your son's eternal destiny was most important to you. But to God, everyone's soul is equally important. And maybe he put you and the professor together so you can help prevent others from ending up just like Jamie."

Jonathon shrugged his shoulders. "I'm really not following you, Pastor."

The pastor explained, "Well, we Christians have succeeded in changing the curriculums taught in many high schools. We have gotten the teaching of creationism placed side-by-side with the damnable theory of evolution. Perhaps God wants to use you to change the humanistic curriculum taught at that professor's university. If you can stop them from spreading lies, from blinding students to the truth, who knows how many souls you can bring to Christ?"

Jonathon pondered the pastor's words as he made his way to the adult Sunday school room.

¤ ¤ ¤

The Sunday school teacher began, "This month is Church History Month. Today we're going to discuss the history behind the most fundamental Christian doctrine: the Trinity—the doctrine that the Father, Son, and Holy Ghost are co-equal and co-eternal."

Jonathon, a highly successful engineering professional, was usually uninterested in history. "This is going to be boring," he thought. "Why does today have to be about history?"

The teacher continued, "The doctrine of the Trinity was developed in the fourth century by Gregory of Nyssa[1], when there were two distinct divisions in Christianity: the Latin churches of the West, and the Greek-speaking churches of the East. Gregory was so revered, so respected, that he was canonized as a saint in both the Western and Eastern churches."

It was as if a bolt of lightning struck Jonathon. "That's it!"

---

1 "Saint Gregory of Nyssa," *Britannica Concise Encyclopedia* (Encyclopædia Britannica, 2007), http://concise.britannica.com/ebc/article-9038037/Gregory-of-Nyssa.

he exclaimed to himself. "I know how I can show that professor he's wrong!" Jonathon was inspired to make it his mission to change the university's curriculum.

It struck Jonathon that, at the start of Christianity, there may have been a few Christians who denied the reality of eternal punishment in hell. And the professor was probably exaggerating the number of such fringe believers in his claim that the original Christians believed all human souls will be reunited with God.

So Jonathon began formulating a plan. He decided to show the professor irrefutable documentation that mainstream, orthodox Christian founders, such as Gregory of Nyssa, taught that sinners would burn in hell forever. He reasoned that even the professor would have to agree that it didn't matter what fringe, unorthodox people believed.

Jonathon pulled out a pen and started making notes about Gregory.

The teacher continued her lesson. "In AD 381 all the major churches of the East and the West got together in Constantinople to develop a unified statement of faith, called the Nicene Creed. Gregory's Trinitarian formula was added to the Nicene Creed at this Second Ecumenical Council[2]—a council in which Gregory played a prominent role.[3] The Constantinople version of the Nicene Creed continues to shape Christianity to this very day, as it it is accepted as authoritative by the Roman Catholic, Eastern Orthodox, Anglican, and major Protestant churches."[4]

"This really is the answer!" Jonathon thought. "Gregory is the key. He was the one who developed the doctrine of the Trinity, and he helped develop the very creed upon which orthodox Christianity is based. After I document that he and other eminent founders believed in the eternal fires of hell, the professor will have to reconsider what he teaches."

Jonathon walked out of the classroom confident with his new

---

2  "Holy Ghost," *The Catholic Encyclopedia*, Volume VII (New York: Robert Appleton Company, 1910).
3  David Hugh Farmer, "Gregory of Nyssa," *The Oxford Dictionary of Saints* (2004)
4  "Nicene Creed." *Encyclopædia Britannica*. 2010. *Encyclopædia Britannica Online. 29 Oct. 2010 <http://www.britannica.com/EBchecked/topic/413955/Nicene-Creed>.

plan.

¤ ¤ ¤

After Sunday school, Jonathon caught Pastor Rick in the foyer. He told the pastor that he had decided to accept the challenge. And then he shared his plan of attack.

Pastor Rick smiled. "I'm glad to hear you are going to follow through on my suggestion. And I particularly like your approach. In fact, a friend of mine is a professor of Christian history at seminary. I can arrange for the two of you to talk this week. I'm sure he'll be able to give you all the information you need to successfully rebut the professor. I think you have a great idea."

"If I can make anything good come out of Jamie's death, I'll do it," Jonathon told him.

¤ ¤ ¤

As Jonathon headed in the direction of the sanctuary, he was intercepted by Mark and Grace. Mark was Jonathon's closest friend, and Grace was Samantha's.

"Hi, Jonathon. Listen, are you and Samantha up for some company yet?" Mark asked.

Jonathon smiled, reflecting on their relationship. The two couples had visited together two or three times every week since the Webbers had moved to San Diego thirty years ago. Their relationship was cemented by their mutual commitment to living life based on the principles of the Bible, which both couples considered to be the only source of truth. They firmly believed that each and every word was supernaturally inspired by God himself.

Turning to Grace, Jonathon said, "I think Samantha really needs your help. She spends most of her time in bed, crying. I don't know what I can do to help her. Maybe she'll reach out to you."

Grace grabbed her husband's hand as she told Jonathon, "I'm sure Mark won't mind if I take some time off work so I could visit

Samantha as often as she wants."

"I think that's a great idea," Mark said. "Why don't we bring some dinner over on Tuesday, and you can make some plans with Samantha?"

"That would be great," Jonathon said. "Look, I'm going to skip the morning service and head on home. I'm concerned about Samantha being there alone. See you on Tuesday."

On the drive home, Jonathon became excited about documenting what prominent Christian founders like Saint Gregory taught about the fate of sinners. He was sure this would put the liberal professor in his place.

But Jonathon's excitement quickly turned to sadness as he thought about his own son. Overcome with grief, he pulled over to the side of the road. Clenching his eyes shut, he said aloud, "Jamie, I love you so much. You cannot even begin to know the pain I feel when I picture you suffering in the fires of hell."

Tears welled up in his eyes. "I just wish to God that you could be purified from your sins, even after death. But no amount of false hope is going to alter the fate of your soul. And I cannot idly stand by and let this professor teach a lie that could send other men and women to the same horrid fate as you."

With his jaw clenched, Jonathon regained his composure and drove the rest of the way home.

# Chapter Four

Peter was released from the hospital Sunday afternoon. A stack of mail, mostly bills, awaited him. It wasn't until he opened the mortgage bill that it dawned on him that the house was in Jamie's name. In his grief, he hadn't considered the new economic reality he now found himself in.

Peter was a struggling artist. After Jamie made partner at the law firm three years ago, Peter quit his job to focus on his painting career—a career well suited for his highly emotional, manic-depressive personality. So far, he hadn't sold a single painting. Now he found himself jobless, penniless, homeless, and alone—dealing with the loss of his best friend and life partner.

Unable to look at the bills any longer, he bundled them up and threw them into a drawer. He walked over to the liquor cabinet, grabbed the scotch, and began to drink—straight from the bottle. Before he could empty it, he passed out cold on the couch.

Peter awoke in the evening with a massive, pounding headache. With his body and mind trashed, he felt even more alone and more depressed. Using his last ounce of willpower, he stood up, splashed water on his face, and headed for Stardust, a local bar.

Peter had struggled with addiction to alcohol long before he met Jamie. Jamie's influence had kept him on the straight and narrow. But with the agony of Jamie's death, he was more desperate than ever to numb himself.

"Give me an Absolut straight up," Peter yelled to the bartender. "A double." He downed the drink, but it didn't do the trick. "You got anything stronger?"

"That's Chuck's job," the bartender half-joked, making a reference to the dealer who supplied drugs to the club's patrons.

"Did I hear my name?" asked a fashionably dressed guy as he leaned on the bar next to Peter.

"You Chuck?" Peter inquired.

"Yep."

"What do you got?"

Chuck hesitated. He had never seen Peter before. After taking a moment to size him up, he asked, "How much do you have on you?"

"About fifty bucks."

Chuck motioned for Peter to follow him as he headed to the restroom.

Chuck entered a toilet stall, leaving the door open. "Come here."

Peter joined Chuck inside.

Chuck closed the stall door. He took Peter's money and pulled out a small plastic bag filled with crystal powder.

"What is it?"

Chuck rolled his eyes. "It's crystal, man!" He lowered his voice, "You know … meth."

"What do I do with it?" Peter asked.

"You can take a key, scoop a little out, and snort it. But if you want to feel really good, you've got to smoke it."

"Thanks," Peter said as he left the stall with the plastic bag deep in his pocket.

After a couple more shots, he went home. Peter found out from the Internet how to prepare the drug for smoking, then, putting what he had learned into practice, he was gone to the world.

¤ ¤ ¤

Jonathon awoke to the ringing alarm clock. "Samantha, honey, today's Tuesday. Remember, Mark and Grace are coming over tonight."

Samantha had spent the week crying, confined to the bedroom. "Okay. I'll straighten up the house," she said in a monotone.

"Don't worry, honey. I've been keeping the house shipshape. You can keep resting. You just have to get yourself ready by six o'clock this evening."

Jonathon kissed his wife on the forehead and then rose to prepare for work. As he rose, his cell phone rang.

"Hello, I'm Frank Wright … from seminary," a voice announced. "Is this Jonathon Webber?"

Jonathon smiled. The pastor's friend had responded quickly. "Yes, and thanks for calling. I've been eager to talk to you."

"What can I do to help you, Jonathon?"

"Well, did Pastor Rick explain my project to you?"

"Not really," Frank replied. "He just told me you needed help finding historical references to refute a misleading liberal class being taught at a university. I'm always ready to help fight the liberal agenda."

Jonathon was relieved to have such a willing ally. "Terrific. What I need is a list of historical documents that contain quotes from the earliest Christian leaders, quotes showing they taught that sinners are punished in hell for all eternity."

"Ah. That'll be easy," Frank said. "That teaching is very well documented, right from the beginning of Christianity onward."

Jonathon grinned relieved to know it would be so easy to show the professor that he was wrong. He pulled out the notes he made from Sunday school and found the name he wrote of the prominent church father who developed the doctrine of the Trinity and helped create the foundational Christian creed. Then he said, "I'd specifically like documentation from the most influential church founders, such as Gregory of Nyssa."

"Are you playing with me, Jonathon?" Frank asked.

"Huh? What do you mean?"

"Well, I'm afraid I can't give you any references specifically from Gregory of Nyssa."

"Why not?"

Frank hesitated. "Well, Gregory believed that all of humanity will spend eternity as God's friends."[5]

---

5 "When it says that God's enemies shall be subjected to God, this is meant that the power of evil shall be taken away, and *they who, on account of their disobedience were called God's enemies, shall by subjection be made God's friends.* When, then, all who were once God's enemies, shall have been made His footstool (because they will then receive in themselves the divine imprint), when death shall have been destroyed;

Jonathon was stunned. "I'm confused. Was this a personal belief, or something he taught publicly?"

"Gregory wrote about this idea in many essays," Frank replied. "He also spoke about it regularly in his homilies.[6] It's something he taught openly and often."

Jonathon raked his fingers through his hair. "I have to say I'm very surprised about all of this."

Frank continued. "You have to realize that at this time in history, many Christian churches believed the heresy of universal salvation—the idea that every soul will be reconciled to God. In fact, only one theological school taught the truth, the one in Rome. All the other Christian theological schools—Alexandria, Antioch, Caesarea, Edessa, and Ephesus—taught that sinners will be punished for a limited amount of time."[7]

Jonathon felt let down. "But you said you can give me a list of leaders, starting from the beginning of Christianity, who taught that sinners will burn in hell forever."

"Oh, yes," Frank confirmed. "And if you want quotes from the fourth century, the time of Saint Gregory of Nyssa, I'd be glad to give you quotes from leaders affiliated with the Roman church."

Jonathon was completely thrown. "But that doesn't help me at all. I was trying to come up with information to refute the professor's claim that the original Christians believed everyone will get to heaven. But you're telling me the majority of the early orthodox theological schools actually did teach that."

"Jonathon, there was so much going on during that time in history. And I'm afraid I'm confusing you more than helping you. Maybe the best approach would be for the secular professor to speak directly with me."

---

in the subjection of all, which is not servile humility, but immortality and Christ is said by the apostle Paul to be made subject to God"—Oratory in I Cor. xv.28, Saint Gregory of Nyssa. Emphasis added.

6 "Now the body of Christ, *as I have said often before*, is the whole of humanity"—Oratory in I Cor. xv.28, Saint Gregory of Nyssa. Emphasis added.

7 "In the first five or six centuries of Christianity there were six known theological schools, of which *four (Alexandria, Antioch, Caesarea and Edessa) were Universalist, one (Ephesus) accepted conditional immortality; one (Carthage or Rome) taught endless punishment of the wicked."*—"Universalists," *Schaff Herzog Encyclopedia of Religious Knowledge* (1912). Emphasis added.

"Are you sure that won't be too much trouble?" Jonathon asked as some of the tension began to drain from his body.

Frank assured him. "Your pastor and I were close friends at seminary. He knows how much I enjoy putting liberal academics in their place. I'm sure that's why he referred you to me. And Jonathon, I have to say, I almost always win."

Jonathon considered the offer for a moment and then replied. "Well, I promised God that I'd give this project 100 percent, and you seem really confident. And the professor did ask me to call him. I'll see if I can set something up. I have to go now. I'm already late for a meeting."

Jonathon hurriedly got ready for work and headed off to his office.

While he was driving, his confidence started flip-flopping. "I was sure that the professor was crazy to say the early Christians believed every soul would make it to heaven," he thought. "But it looks like he was right ... No, he can't be right; otherwise everyone would already have heard about this before ... Yet there has to be a reason why Saint Gregory, one of the greatest Christian thinkers, believed everyone would be reconciled with God. There must be a reason why five out of six theological schools taught it as well ... But, then again, Frank seemed certain of what he was talking about. After all, he is the expert."

Jonathon stepped out of his car and, dismissing his thoughts, rushed to his meeting.

# Chapter Five

Mark and Grace came over that evening as planned. After dinner, Mark and Jonathon headed for the living room while their wives cleaned up in the kitchen.

Jonathon eagerly explained his new mission to Mark. After he finished describing his conversation with Frank, he said, "I have to admit I was surprised. I've always assumed that the founding church fathers believed the same things that we do in our church. But even though I'm a little confused right now, Frank seemed very confident. I'm sure I must be missing something ... something that will become clear after I get the two professors to talk directly with each other."

Mark nodded. "It would be fun to be a fly on the wall during that debate! I'd love to watch Frank run circles around that university professor. Make sure you call me after it's over so you can give me a blow-by-blow description."

Jonathon chuckled. "You can count on it."

¤ ¤ ¤

In the kitchen, Samantha burst into tears. "Every time I see the urn containing Jamie's ashes, I'm reminded of his death and his condemnation. Whenever I see it, it's torture."

"I'm sorry for asking this," Grace said softly. "But why did you decide to have him cremated if you knew it was going to cause you so much anguish?"

"I did it to honor Jamie's wishes. He always said if anything happened to him, he didn't want a burial or a funeral. He wanted a private cremation with no one mourning over him."

"I see," was all Grace could say.

Samantha trembled. "Why did God answer our prayers for a son when he knew our child would end up in hell? God knew Jamie's destiny before he was born, yet he gave him to us anyway."

Grace gently placed her hand on Samantha's trembling shoulder.

Samantha continued, "It would have been better if my son had never been born at all."

Grace remained silent.

With tears streaming down her face, Samantha moaned, "I hate to say it, but I think I may need to see a doctor for my depression. I feel like there's a dark cloud hanging over me all the time."

Grace pointed her finger at Samantha. "Bite your tongue! You don't need to see a shrink who'll just put you on medication and turn you into a zombie. You just need to have greater faith in Jesus. You need to trust the Holy Spirit to give you the comfort and strength you need to go through this."

Samantha's cheeks reddened. "I know you're right, but I feel like I'm failing God. Sometimes, in the mornings, I wish I wouldn't ever have to wake up again."

"Then I'll pray even harder for you to experience the comfort of the Holy Spirit," Grace said. "I'll also ask God to guide me on how I can help you. And remember, I'm always here for you."

¤ ¤ ¤

Peter hadn't slept since smoking the crystal meth three evenings ago. He promised himself that using the drug was going to be a one-time experience. There was no way he would ever allow himself to feel this lousy again.

Although Peter knew he should focus on looking for a job and a new place to live, he was simply too exhausted. So he dragged himself to the bedroom, laid down, and fell asleep.

¤ ¤ ¤

That same morning, Jonathon found the card the professor had given him at the hospital. "DONALD RICHMOND, PhD," the card read.

"A liberal PhD, no wonder the professor's messed up," Jonathon said to himself as he dialed the number on the card.

"I don't know if you remember me; we met at Holy Cross Hospital," Jonathon said by way of introduction. The memory of that day so overwhelmed him that he started stuttering. "M-my unsaved son … died in a car accident that day."

"Yes, I remember. Jonathon, right?"

"Yes. I …" Jonathon stammered. "You asked me to contact you if I wanted to discuss my religious beliefs."

"I remember," Dr. Richmond replied. "What's on your mind?"

Jonathon explained. "At the hospital, you made a comment that the original Christians believed every human soul would inherit eternal life with God. I talked to a Christian history professor about your statement, and I got a little confused by his response. He thought it would be helpful for me if you guys thrash through your differences on a three-way conference call so I can learn from your exchange."

The professor hesitated. "So he wants to debate me, huh?"

"Well, I don't know if you'd call it a debate. Maybe a vigorous discussion would be a better way to put it."

"Jonathon, I'm glad you called. But although I want to help, I really don't want to debate a narrow-minded, highly indoctrinated, religious conservative, so-called educator."

Jonathon thought, "Look who's talking—a narrow-minded, totally brainwashed, atheistic liberal so-called doctor." Not wanting to be argumentative, he simply kept quiet.

The professor continued. "I'm sorry, Jonathon, but I'm going to have to turn down your offer. How are you and your wife doing?"

Jonathon sighed, feeling deflated. "I keep myself as busy as possible to avoid thinking about everything. But my wife, Samantha, is terribly depressed. I'm very concerned about her. She's hardly left the bedroom since we got home from San Francisco. She blames herself for our son's rejection of Christ. She believes he's in hell because she didn't do enough."

Professor Richmond paused. "I'm so sorry to hear that ... Jonathon, I'd be glad to do anything I can to help you and your wife heal. And if talking to your friend will help, then I'm willing to do that for you. Why don't you see about setting up that teleconference?"

"Terrific! What about Friday evening?"

"That'd be fine."

"I'll check with Frank, the Christian history professor I told you about. And I'll confirm by e-mail."

¤ ¤ ¤

On Wednesday afternoon, Grace came to visit Samantha. Samantha smiled and welcomed her friend inside.

After they were seated in the living room, Grace said, "I've been thinking ... maybe reading some words from the scriptures might help comfort you. In fact, I came over here with a specific passage in mind."

Samantha sat up straight, feeling a twinge of hope. "Thank you. That sounds like a great idea."

Samantha grabbed her favorite Bible (the NASB translation) and asked which passage Grace wanted them to read.

"Let's read a passage from the book written by Jesus's disciple Luke. Let's read Luke, chapter four, verses seventeen and eighteen."

After Samantha found the passage, Grace read it aloud: "And the book of the prophet Isaiah was handed to [Jesus]. And He opened the book and found the place where it was written,

> The spirit of the Lord is upon me,
> Because He anointed me to preach the gospel to the poor.
> He has sent me to proclaim release to the captives,
> And recovery of sight to the blind,
> TO SET FREE THOSE WHO ARE OPPRESSED."

When they were done, Grace looked up. "You see, whenever we are down and out, it's always good to remember that Jesus came to free us from whatever is oppressing us."

Samantha appreciated her friend's attempt. However, the little pep talk wasn't even making a dent in her depression. "This is a nice reminder. Thank you."

Samantha looked at the page where those words were written. She noticed that the footnote said that Jesus was reading from the sixty-first chapter of the book of Isaiah (one of the books from the Jewish scriptures that is included in the Christian Bible). "Grace, let's go to the sixty-first chapter of Isaiah, the chapter where Luke said Jesus was reading from."

Samantha and Grace both flipped to the sixty-first chapter of Isaiah. Grace read the entire chapter silently to herself. When she finished, she looked up and saw Samantha staring at her Bible with a bewildered look on her face. "Samantha, what's wrong?"

"Grace, this is really strange. The words written in Isaiah aren't the same words that Jesus read."

"What do you mean?" Grace asked. "They look the same to me."

"Here, let me show you." Samantha took out a piece of paper and drew a line down the middle. She labeled the left half "The words Luke said Jesus read from Isaiah" and the right half "The words written in the book of Isaiah." Then she copied the words from Luke side-by-side with the words from Isaiah:

| *The words Luke said that Jesus read from Isaiah* | *The words written in the book of Isaiah* |
|---|---|
| The Spirit of the Lord is upon me, | The Spirit of the Lord God is upon me, |
| Because He anointed me to preach the Gospel to the poor, | Because the Lord has anointed me to bring good news to the afflicted, |
| [missing] | **He has sent me to bind up the brokenhearted,** |
| He has sent me to proclaim release to the captives, | To proclaim liberty to the captives, |
| **And recovery of sight to the blind,** | [missing] |
| To set free those who are oppressed. | And freedom to prisoners. |

Samantha pointed to her chart. "See, the book of Isaiah mentions 'the brokenhearted', but those words are missing from what Luke said Jesus read. Also, Luke said that Jesus read the words 'recovery of sight to the blind', yet those words are missing from the book of Isaiah."

Grace sighed. "Well, the differences don't seem too important."

"Yes, but the scriptures are inspired word-for-word by God," Samantha retorted. "And I used to study from the NASB version because I thought that it was accurately translated word-for-word. I didn't realize there were entire phrases mismatched in this translation."

Grace rolled her eyes. "You and Jonathon are always so analytical."

Samantha understood what her friend meant. Samantha had been one of the few female students at the engineering college where she had met Jonathon. Their love of the Bible combined with their passion for all things analytical had created a special bond between them.

As a highly trained engineer, Samantha couldn't let the discrepancy pass by without understanding why it existed. She stood up, went into the den, and opened another copy of the Bible, this one a King James translation. To her amazement it contained the very same discrepancy: only Isaiah mentioned "the brokenhearted," and only Luke mentioned "the blind." So she grabbed yet another translation— the NIV—only to become even more surprised; it too had the exact differences. She tossed the NIV onto the desk and went back into the living room.

"Grace, the three most popular translations of the Bible—the NIV, the NASB, and the KJV—all have the exact same contradiction. How can this be?"

"Why don't you find out why they're different?" Grace encouraged. "I'm sure someone must have written about it."

"I will. It just seems so odd."

While Grace seemed to easily shrug off the contradiction, Samantha felt there had to be a profoundly important reason why the quotes were different. After all, she was always taught that the words of the Bible were exact, word for word. Yet she knew it was impossible for both Luke and Isaiah to be correct on a word-for-word basis, given their differences.

Samantha sat with a puzzled look on her face. "Which one has the right words, Luke or Isaiah? And why do all the translations have the same exact contradiction?"

And when the implications of her questions hit her, the intrigue gave way to worry. "Something is terribly wrong."

# Chapter Six

Peter woke from his fitful sleep Wednesday evening. Although he hadn't eaten in a couple days, there was only one thing he really wanted—more crystal meth.

If Peter had snorted the meth, he probably wouldn't have become addicted so quickly. But by smoking it, he quickly experienced a degree of physical dependency.

Not even bothering to shower or eat, Peter headed straight for Stardust. He found Chuck at the club, made his purchase, and then went home to smoke.

¤ ¤ ¤

On Wednesday night, Samantha decided to restart her habit of reading the Bible before falling asleep. Normally, she would read from the NASB translation. But as she walked into the den, she noticed the NIV translation she had left on the desk. So she picked it up, went into the bedroom, and joined Jonathon under the sheets.

Still bothered by the Isaiah/Luke conflict, she once again flipped to the sixty-first chapter of Isaiah. This time, she noticed that a footnote in the NIV translation contained an explanation: "brokenhearted" was in the Hebrew version, whereas "blind" was in the Septuagint.

Ever since childhood, Samantha had been taught that Jesus and his disciples read from a Hebrew version of the Jewish scriptures. Yet the NIV's footnote indicated the words Jesus read are not found in the Hebrew version of the Jewish scriptures. Rather, the NIV footnote says the words Jesus read are found in something called 'a Septuagint.'

Rather than closing the case, the NIV's footnote only generated more questions. "What is a Septuagint?" she wondered. "Luke said that Jesus read the word 'blind.' So Jesus must have been reading this Septuagint thing, not the Hebrew scriptures that are used in my Bible … But that's strange. Because if Jesus read from a Septuagint and not the Hebrew, then why aren't any of my Bibles translated from this Septuagint? Why aren't my Bibles translated from the same scriptures that Jesus used?"

Samantha turned to Jonathon. "Honey, have you ever heard of something called a Septuagint?"

"No, dear, why do you ask?"

"It's a new word I heard today. I'll look it up tomorrow."

"Okay, honey." Jonathon yawned. "Wake me if you need anything."

"Good night, dear. I love you."

"I love you, too, sweetheart."

¤ ¤ ¤

Samantha woke with one thought on her mind: "What is a Septuagint?" While Jonathon got ready for work, she went straight to the den to get a copy of the *American Heritage Dictionary*. She found the entry for Septuagint:

> **Sep·tu·a·gint** (sĕp'tōō-ə-jĭnt', sĕp-tōō'ə-jənt, -tyōō'-) n. A Greek version of the Hebrew Scriptures that dates from the 3rd century B.C., containing both a translation of the Hebrew and additional and variant material, regarded as the standard form of the Old Testament in the early Christian Church and still canonical in the Eastern Orthodox Church.

Samantha was so taken aback by the dictionary entry that she reread the definition five times to make sure she understood it correctly. She knew the Jewish scripture section of her Bible (a section called the Old Testament) was translated from a Hebrew version of the Jewish scriptures—the same scriptures she was taught that Jesus used. She was surprised to discover that a Greek version called the Septuagint served as the standard scripture for the early Church. She had never even heard of the Greek Septuagint version of the Jewish scriptures before.

"That doesn't make sense," she thought. "I have already seen that the Septuagint and the Hebrew aren't the same on a word-for-word basis. So if Jesus considered the Greek Septuagint to be the precise words of God, then how come none of my Bibles are translated from that version?"

Samantha took it a step further. "The dictionary doesn't specifically say that Jesus considered the Septuagint to be scripture," she reasoned. "And the book of Luke only said Jesus read from the Septuagint version of Isaiah. While this might strongly imply that Jesus considered the Septuagint to contain the divinely inspired words of scripture, it doesn't explicitly prove it. So how can I be absolutely certain which version Jesus considered to contain the words of God?"

Samantha was determined to find the answer.

¤ ¤ ¤

On Friday evening, Jonathon anxiously dialed into the conference call and waited for the other two to arrive. "Frank Wright here."

"I'm here too," said Dr. Richmond.

After Jonathon introduced the two men, he smiled. The moment had finally arrived. "Gentlemen, thank you both for agreeing to this conference call. I'm hoping I'll learn a lot from your dialogue."

Dr. Richmond began the debate. "Frank, are you intimately familiar with the history of universal salvation—the doctrine that every soul eventually returns to God?"

Frank answered. "I teach my students the history of all the major heresies, including universal salvation."

"Well, I'm glad you teach your students about it," Dr. Richmond replied. "Given that virtually all the original Christians believed it."

"That's quite an oversimplification, I must say," Frank rebutted.

"If I'm oversimplifying, please, why don't you enlighten me?"

Frank didn't even hesitate for a moment. "The original founders of Christianity taught that sinners get what they deserve—to rot in hell for all eternity. The heresy that every soul unites with God was not introduced to Christianity until the third century. It was first taught by Origen, the head of the Christian theological school at Alexandria."

Dr. Richmond sounded incredulous. "So you teach your seminary students that before the third century, Christians exclusively taught the doctrine of eternal punishment?"

"Of course," Frank replied.

Dr. Richmond continued. "But Frank, the earliest records of any definitive church teachings regarding the length of punishment are from the second century, right?"

"Yes, that's correct."

"And aren't there second century[8] Christian documents that teach universal salvation, documents such as the Alexandrian Christian homilies, the *Sibylline Oracles?*"[9]

"Uh, well ... yes, I've heard of them," Frank admitted.

Dr. Richmond pressed on. "So if the teaching of universal salvation dates back to the second century, how can you teach your students it was introduced to Christianity by Origen in the third century? How can you say that Origen started the idea of universal salvation in the third century when it was already being taught before he was even born?"

Frank countered. "All right, maybe Origen didn't start universal salvation per se. But he did introduce a heretical way of interpreting the scriptures. He taught that the scriptures shouldn't be interpreted literally. Instead, he taught a non-literal, allegorical method of scripture interpretation. And it was this non-literal way of interpreting scripture that led many churches in the East astray."

Dr. Richmond paused. "So you're saying the only reason the early Christians in the East believed in universal salvation was because they took an allegorical, non-literal approach to interpreting the Bible?

8  "the prophecies were actually the work of certain Jewish and Christian writers *from about 150 BC to about AD 180*—"Sibylline Oracles," *Encyclopædia Britannica Online* (Encyclopædia Britannica, 2007), http://www.britannica.com/eb/article-9067614. Emphasis added.

9  "To these pious ones the imperishable God, the universal ruler, will also give another thing. *Whenever they ask the imperishable God to save men from the raging fire and deathless gnashing he will grant it, and he will do this. For he will pick them out again from the undying fire and set them elsewhere ...*"—*Sibylline Oracle* 2:330–338. Emphasis added.

An approach they learned from Origen?"

"Well, of course," Frank confidently responded. "If the scriptures are taken literally, at face value, then anyone would have to accept the reality of hell's eternal existence."

"Then how do you explain the Eastern theological school of Antioch?"

"What do you mean?" Frank asked rather dismissively.

Dr. Richmond answered with a slightly sarcastic tone, "Well, Frank, wasn't the Antioch school known for its insistence on a very strict literal interpretation of the scriptures? Wasn't it even founded in opposition to Origen and his allegorical school?"[10]

"Yes," Frank mumbled weakly.

"So then why don't *you* tell Jonathon what the Antioch school, the one dedicated to a literal interpretation of the scriptures, taught regarding the fate of sinners?" Dr. Richmond insisted.

There was total silence for about twenty seconds.

"Okay," Frank finally said. "The theological school in Antioch taught that the souls of sinners will receive eternal life after being purified in the fires of hell."[11, 12]

"So now we agree on two things," Dr. Richmond proudly declared. "We agree that the doctrine of universal salvation is found in the earliest Christian literature, and it was taught by allegorical and literal theological schools alike."

Frank balked. "Doc, your little summary is only true of the theological schools of the East. The reality of eternal damnation in hell was always maintained in the West."

---

10 "Christian theological institution in Syria, traditionally founded in about AD 200, that *stressed the literal interpretation of the Bible* and the completeness of Christ's humanity, *in opposition to the School of Alexandria* (see Alexandria, School of), which emphasized the allegorical interpretation of the Bible and stressed Christ's divinity."—"Antioch, School of," *Encyclopædia Britannica Online* (Encyclopædia Britannica, 2007), http://www.britannica.com/eb/article-9007857. Emphasis added.

11 Theodore of Mopsuestia [was a] Syrian theologian and spiritual head of the school of Antioch. ... He is said to have introduced into the Nestorian church the doctrine of universal salvation.—"Theodore of Mopsuestia," *Britannica Concise Encyclopedia* (Encyclopædia Britannica, 2007), http://www.britannica.com/ebc/article-9380569.

12 "*That in the world to come, those who have done evil all their life long, will be made worthy of the sweetness of the Divine bounty. For never would Christ have said 'Until thou hast paid the uttermost farthing,' unless it were possible for us to be cleansed when we have paid our debts.*"—Theodore of Mopsuestia, Head of the School of Antioch, Fragment iv. Emphasis added.

"What?" Dr. Richmond asked. "Are you not familiar with an early second-century book entitled *The Apocalypse of Peter*?"

"A little," Frank responded.

"Well, another second century document, called the Muratorian Fragment, records that *The Apocalypse of Peter* was widely read in the churches of the West,"[13] Dr. Richmond explained.

"And your point is?" Frank asked.

"My point is simple," Dr. Richmond replied. "In *The Apocalypse of Peter*, God releases the souls from hell at the request of the Christians.[14, 15] The book taught universal salvation—showing many Western churches must have also embraced universal salvation from the very beginning of Christianity."

Frank winced. "I guess it's possible that *some* of the first Western Christians were misled. But you have to admit that *most* Christians in the West never believed it."

"Frank, what history books do you read?" Dr. Richmond asked. "In the early fifth century, didn't Saint Augustine lament in *Enchiridion* that 'indeed *most persons* deplore the eternal punishment, and perpetual, uninterrupted torments of the lost, and say they do not believe it shall be so'?[16] Didn't he write that the *majority* of Christians in Rome, the very heart of Western Christianity, believed that the punishment of sinners will be temporary?"

"Uh … yes. He did write that," Frank conceded.

Dr. Richmond asserted, "So archaeology has revealed the *Sibylline Oracles* were very popular in the second century churches of the East and *The Apocalypse of Peter* was very popular in the second century churches of the West, documenting that the teaching of

---

13  "Biblical literature," *Encyclopædia Britannica Online* (Encyclopædia Britannica, 2007), http://www.britannica.com/eb/article-73390.

14  Then I shall give unto my called and my chosen whomsoever they shall ask me for, out of torment, and will give them a fair baptism unto salvation—*Apocalypse of Peter*, 14.

15  "This much is certain: The earlier versions of the text [of *The Apocalypse of Peter*], originating in the second century, envisioned the posthumous salvation of at least some wicked sinners at the last judgment,"—Jeffery Trumbower, *Rescue for the Dead: The Posthumous Salvation of Non-Christians in Early Christianity* (Oxford: Oxford University Press, 2001), 51.

16  "It is in vain, then, that some, indeed *most [persons]*, make moan over the eternal punishment, and perpetual, uninterrupted torments of the lost, *and say they do not believe it shall be so*"—Augustine, *The Enchiridion*, Chapter 112, first sentence, Emphasis added.

universal salvation was widespread in the earliest churches of both the East and the West. And Saint Augustine's *Enchiridion* documents that the teaching of universal salvation remained the mainstream Christian belief up into the beginning of the fifth century—despite the official teachings of the Roman theological school. In other words, it's just as I said at the very beginning of this conversation, *virtually all the original orthodox Christians embraced the doctrine of universal salvation.*"

The line remained totally silent for almost a minute. Finally, Frank broke the silence. "I simply cannot agree to characterize it that way," he said. "Jonathon, it's very clear that Dr. Richmond knows how to use a lot of doubletalk to box me into a corner. And it's also obvious that he and I are operating from different sets of assumptions. I don't see how it would be useful to continue this conversation."

Jonathon was totally confused, but he responded the only way he could. "Okay. Well, thanks for your time. Both of you."

With that, Frank hung up the phone, leaving Jonathon and Dr. Richmond on the line.

Dr. Richmond started speaking. "Jonathon, don't hold anything against Frank. He's simply regurgitating something he likely learned when he was in seminary. In fact, the idea of setting up Origen as the straw man of universal salvation dates all the way back to the fifth century to a man named Jerome."[17] Dr. Richmond hesitated for a moment. His voice took on a very serious tone as he said, "And, Jonathon, there is something very important I need to tell you about Jerome. Jerome—"

Jonathon cut the professor off. "Professor, I apologize, but my head is more than full right now. I really appreciate your time. Thank you."

"You're welcome, Jonathon. I hope this was helpful."

"It was. And it was generous of you to agree to it."

"My pleasure. Take care, Jonathon."

---

17 "[Origen] also allowed that in the end all might be saved, a view that particularly shocked St Jerome: 'Origen *teaches* that after many ages and one restoration of all things, Gabriel will be in the same state as the devil, Paul as Caiaphas, and virgins as prostitutes.'"—"Origen," *The Oxford Dictionary of Philosophy* (Oxford: Oxford University Press, 2005). Emphasis added.
NOTE: Notice how Jerome ascribes the teaching of Universal Salvation to Origen (even though the teaching predates Origen's birth).

The two men hung up the phone.

Jonathon's mind was numb. The debate had played out very differently than he expected.

# Chapter Seven

On Saturday afternoon, Peter came down from yet another two-day crystal meth high. He could hardly believe that almost a whole week had passed since Jamie had died. The house was a wreck. He was a bigger wreck. He dragged himself to the bedroom and crashed.

◻ ◻ ◻

When Mark and Grace arrived at the Webbers' on Saturday, Samantha couldn't wait to talk about her discovery. "Remember our Bible study the other day where Luke said Jesus read the words 'recovery of sight to the blind' in the book of Isaiah?"

"Yes."

"Well, it turns out those words are not in the Hebrew version of the Jewish scriptures. Those words are in a Greek version of the Jewish scriptures, called the Septuagint. And since Jesus read those words, then he must have been reading from the Septuagint, a different version of the Jewish scriptures than the ones used in the Old Testament section of our Bibles. Isn't that interesting?"

"It is," Grace concurred.

Samantha continued. "But what bothers me is: Did Jesus consider the Greek Septuagint to be the inspired Word of God? And— Samantha suddenly stopped, a look of excitement beaming from her face. "Of course! I've just figured it out! It will be easy to find out which version Jesus considered to be authentic!"

Grace looked taken aback. "What are you talking about?"

Samantha explained. "All we have to do is to find places in the Bible where Jesus quotes from the Jewish scriptures. If his quotes match the Hebrew scriptures used in our Bible, then that must be the version Jesus considered to represent the words of God. But if Jesus's quotes match the Septuagint, then that must be the one!"

"That's a great idea. Let me know what you find out. By the way, are you going to church tomorrow?"

Samantha hung her head. "No. You're the only person I'm up to seeing right now. Maybe I'll start attending services next week."

Grace hugged her friend. "I understand."

¤ ¤ ¤

Mark was watching football in the living room with Jonathon while his wife visited with Samantha. "So, Jonathon, you haven't told me about the battle between the two professors."

Jonathon was hoping Mark had forgotten about it. "Well, I have to say it didn't go anything like the way I thought it would."

"What happened?" Mark asked.

A defeated look came upon Jonathon's face. "If I had to judge the debate, I'd have to say the liberal professor won. You know, it's funny, but I felt like Dorothy in *The Wizard of Oz*. She thought the wizard was this giant, powerful being—until she pulled back the curtain and saw the little munchkin of a man. That's exactly how I felt about Frank. He's one of the top historical experts in our church, but Dr. Richmond's references completely squashed Frank's characterization of church history. I always thought the experts in our denomination had everything pretty much figured out."

Mark sternly replied. "But, Jonathon, remember, just because someone's a good debater, it doesn't mean their conclusions are correct. Maybe that liberal professor is simply a better talker."

"Yeah, I've thought about that," Jonathon muttered unconvincingly.

¤ ¤ ¤

The moment Mark got home he headed straight to the phone to call Pastor Rick.

"I'm concerned about Jonathon," he told the pastor. "I think this whole mission to convert the professor is affecting his walk with Christ. That smart-talking liberal professor outmaneuvered your friend Frank, and it's really shaken Jonathon."

"I'll give Frank a call this evening to find out what happened. Don't worry, I'll get to the bottom of this and follow up with Jonathon," the pastor assured him.

¤ ¤ ¤

Peter awoke Saturday night and realized his cravings for another hit of crystal meth were getting out of control. "Who cares if I am addicted?" he asked himself.

He opened the nightstand and withdrew fifty dollars from Jamie's stash of five hundred. Then he headed out to Stardust once again.

¤ ¤ ¤

Jonathon and Samantha awoke at the same time Sunday morning.

"Are you going to church?" Jonathon asked.

"No, honey. Not today. I'm not ready to answer everyone's questions about what happened."

Jonathon gently stroked his wife's arm. "I understand, and I know the people in the church do, too."

Samantha rose from the bed. "And please don't worry about me being alone this morning. I have my own Bible study already planned for today." She couldn't wait to research Jesus's quotes.

Jonathon smiled. "I'm very glad to hear that, dear," he said as he got out of bed. "Well, I'd better get myself ready for church."

"I can make breakfast," Samantha offered brightly. It was the first meal that she had volunteered to make since Jamie had passed on.

The moment Jonathon left, Samantha began her analysis. She decided to examine every place in the Bible where Jesus quoted the book of Isaiah, the same biblical book she and Grace read from the other day.

To do her analysis, Samantha divided pieces of paper into three sections. She wrote Jesus's quotes of Isaiah in the middle section. On the left she copied the words from the book of Isaiah in her Bible. On the right, she used the footnotes in the NIV translation to reconstruct the words found in the Septuagint. Then she noted each place where one version of Jewish scriptures agreed more with Jesus's quote than the other.

For example, some of Samantha's entries looked like:

| My Bible's book of Isaiah | Jesus's Quote | Septuagint's book of Isaiah |
|---|---|---|
| Isaiah 6:10 | Matthew 13:15 | Isaiah 6:10 |
| Make the heart of this people calloused; | For the heart of this people **has become** dull, | This people's heart **has become** calloused; |
| Make their ears dull | with their ears they **scarcely hear,** | They **hardly hear** with their ears, |
| and close their eyes. | and **they have closed** their eyes, | And **they have closed** their eyes |

| My Bible's book of Isaiah | Jesus's Quote | Septuagint's book of Isaiah |
|---|---|---|
| Isaiah 29:13 | Mark 7:7 | Isaiah 29:13 |
| Their worship of me | But **in vain** do they worship me, | They worship me **in vain;** |
| is made up only of rules taught by men. | **teaching** as doctrines the precepts of men. | **their teachings** are but rules taught by men. |

When Samantha examined the entries she created, she realized that Jesus's quotes agreed with the Greek Septuagint, not the Hebrew translation used in her Bible.

"I don't know what to make of this," she pondered. "So far, the passages I've examined in the Septuagint seem pretty close to the words in my Bible anyway. But could there be passages where the two versions are very different? And even if they are very similar, our Church teaches that every word in the Bible is inspired by God. I've heard many sermons about the meanings of the precise words used in the Bible. Yet now I know those preachers based their sermons on an Old Testament section of the Bible that contains different words than the one Jesus taught from. I really don't know how to sort all this out."

# Chapter Eight

After Sunday school, Pastor Rick rushed to the foyer to catch Jonathon.

"Listen, Jonathon, I talked to Frank last night, and he told me you guys had a very rough go around with the university professor."

Jonathon grimaced. "Yeah, you could say that."

The pastor placed his hand on Jonathon's shoulder. "Frank filled me in on the details. Do you mind if I give you some advice?"

"Not at all, Pastor."

"I think you and Frank approached this from the wrong perspective," the pastor explained. "That's why you got sideswiped."

"What do you mean?"

The pastor clarified. "Jonathon, you guys focused too much on what the early Christians believed, which doesn't really matter at all. It wouldn't matter even if 99 percent of the early Christians taught something, if what they taught contradicts the word of God. The only thing that matters is what *Jesus* taught. You and Frank took the historical bait. That's how the professor snagged you."

It was as if a two-by-four hit Jonathon between the eyes. "Wow! You know … you're right! I don't know why I didn't see it before."

The pastor chuckled. "Sometimes we get so close to things that it's easy to get misled. I was thinking … what would you think about my mentoring you through this mission of yours?"

"I'd really appreciate that."

¤ ¤ ¤

Jonathon met Pastor Rick in his study promptly after the service.

Pastor Rick began. "Did you show the professor passages from

40

the Bible where Jesus says that the unrighteous will be cast into the everlasting lake of fire when he returns to earth?"

"No," Jonathon replied. "But I don't think that will convince him anyway."

"Why not? Jesus's words are stated so clearly."

"I've seen how this guy operates. I can already hear him saying something like, 'Yeah, that's what your Bible says in English, but Jesus's words weren't written in English. They were written in Greek.'"

Pastor Rick appeared to be startled. "So you think this guy might challenge the way the Bible has been translated?"

"I think he'll use any wiggle room he can to avoid seeing the truth."

The pastor shook his head. "It's amazing how stubborn some people can be."

"Yeah," Jonathon said. "We have to show the professor something simple … something so compact that there isn't any wiggle room."

After a long period of silence, the pastor smiled deviously. "If it's Greek he wants, then it's Greek he'll get!"

Jonathon grinned. "What are you thinking?"

"I agree with you, we need something short and sweet—and we need it in the same language Jesus is quoted in. Jesus's disciple Matthew records in his book of the Bible that Jesus used the precise phrase 'eternal punishment' to describe the final destination of sinners."

"Yeah, so?"

"So here's my plan: First, we look up the phrase 'eternal punishment' in the Greek manuscript to find out which Greek words comprise the phrase. Then we take this simple phrase to the good doctor and ask him to have a language professor at his university translate it for him. When his very own colleague tells him it means 'eternal punishment,' we inform him this was the phrase Jesus used to describe the fate of sinners. He'll have no wiggle room. If he's a rational man, he'll be forced to acknowledge his defeat."

"I don't know how much patience this guy's going to have with me," Jonathon said. "He's already completed a long conference call on my behalf. Asking him to get something translated might be asking too much."

Pastor Rick disagreed. "It seems to me that this fellow has an axe to grind against Christianity. Otherwise, why else would he already have spent so much time trying to upset your faith? And this makes me think he must habitually attack the faith of others as well."

After considering the pastor's words, Jonathon concurred. "He does seem awfully motivated to get me to change my mind, which only makes me even more determined to convert him before he damages someone else's faith. It seems very clear to me why God put him in my path. Do you have any reference books here in your study that could show us the phrase 'eternal punishment' in Greek?"

The pastor grabbed an Interlinear New Testament—a version of the Bible written in the original Greek with the English equivalent of each word written underneath. "I studied Greek in seminary, of course, and this is the text we used." He found the passage. "Here it is. Matthew records that Jesus called the fires of hell 'aionios kolasis'— which is Greek for 'eternal punishment.'"

Jonathon copied the phrase 'aionios kolasis' letter for letter.

"Oh yeah, don't forget to ask for the words to be translated from Hellenistic Greek. That's the version of Greek the New Testament was written in. We can't let even the smallest detail slip, or the professor will likely use it against us."

Jonathon made a note to himself. "Got it."

¤ ¤ ¤

On Sunday evening, toward the end of dinner, Samantha listened to Jonathon's new approach toward the professor. "Honey," she said, "don't be too disappointed if the professor doesn't follow through on getting your Greek phrase translated."

"If God wants me to get through to him, he'll open the door," Jonathon replied. "I've got to leave this in his hands." Jonathon rose to get some dessert from the kitchen.

¤ ¤ ¤

Jonathon didn't waste any time Monday morning before calling the professor and asking him to have the Hellenistic Greek phrase 'aionios kolasis' translated. To his surprise, the professor didn't put up any resistance, nor did he even ask why.

"God must be moving this along," Jonathon thought. "Hallelujah."

¤ ¤ ¤

As soon as Dr. Donald Richmond hung up the phone, he called a colleague of his, a doctor of linguistics. "Listen, Charles, I have a favor to ask you. I have a pesky but well-intentioned guy who asked me to have a Greek phrase translated. I assume it's related to some soul-searching he's been doing since his son died in a tragic car accident. I really feel sorry for him and his wife, and if this little task helps him out, that would be great."

"You've always had a bleeding heart, Don," Charles remarked. "How much translating does he want?"

"Just a two-word phrase written in Greek—Hellenistic Greek, to be precise," Dr. Richmond replied.

"That's fine. Should only take me a couple minutes. All the known Greek manuscripts from the Hellenistic period are being digitized so they can be electronically searched. I can go online to perseus.org and cross-reference it in seconds."

"Thanks, Charles. The Hellenistic Greek phrase is 'aionios kolasis.'"

"Easy enough. I'll e-mail you the results at the end of day."

¤ ¤ ¤

That evening, Dr. Richmond logged into his computer before leaving the university. He noticed an e-mail waiting in his inbox from Charles. He opened and read it. "Very interesting," he thought. He added a little note and then forwarded the e-mail to Jonathon.

¤ ¤ ¤

Later that night, Jonathon found the e-mail from Dr. Richmond. Nothing could have prepared him for the contents of the e-mail. He became so upset that he started shaking. "No!" he shouted out loud. "This can't be right! There must be some mistake!"

After Jonathon closed the e-mail, he sat in dazed silence for several minutes.

# Chapter Nine

Visibly shaken and disturbed, Jonathon got up and went to the bedroom.

"What's wrong, honey?" his wife asked him.

"It's … it's just that I'm going to give up trying to convert that professor. That's all. I'm through."

"Why? What happened?"

"I'm too upset to talk about it."

Samantha was worried about her husband giving up. She had seen how the project helped him deal with the loss of their son. "If only there was some way I could help," she mused. Then it hit her like a ton of bricks. "Oh, of course there's a way I can help!"

Samantha had assumed from the look on Jonathon's face that the university professor had refused to look up the Greek phrase. She thought, "If that professor really knows the history of Christianity as well as he claims, then he knows that Jesus and his disciples considered the Greek Septuagint to be the inspired word of God. I'm going to surprise Jonathon and find out if the Septuagint uses the two words he wrote down. And if it does, I can give him undeniable historical proof for the meaning of Jesus's words, proof that the professor cannot ignore."

Samantha needed to buy a little time to see if her plan would work. "Honey, why don't you wait a couple days before deciding whether to end this project or not? Pray about it. I know you are upset now, but maybe God has a way of turning things around."

Jonathon sighed. "I don't see how anything's going to change. But I'll wait a couple days. After all, it's going to be hard to face the pastor and tell him I've failed."

Samantha comforted her husband. "Good night, honey. Hang

in there."

"Good night."

¤ ¤ ¤

The next morning, after Jonathon left for work, Samantha went into the den, fiercely determined to help her husband. Sitting down at the computer, she conducted an Internet search for "Septuagint aionios." Within seconds, more than a thousand results to her query popped up on the computer screen.

Quickly moving beyond her surprise at the numerous entries, Samantha started clicking on them one by one. Eventually she came across a Web site for the Church of the Apostolic Fathers, a church located very close to her home. "This is perfect," she thought. "The pastor of this church has a PhD in language studies from an evangelical university."

Samantha dialed the contact number on the Web site, introduced herself, and presented her question to Reverend Jenkins. "I was wondering if you wouldn't mind answering some Bible questions for me related to the Greek language."

"That's my favorite topic," the reverend replied. "In fact, I did both my master's and doctorate on the theological implications of biblical Greek linguistics."

"That's terrific!" Samantha exclaimed. "I was wondering if you might be able to help me understand some Greek words as they are used in the Septuagint."

"Unfortunately, I'm on my way out and don't have a lot of time at this moment. But if you could come by the church tomorrow afternoon, I'll be glad to answer any questions you may have. Two o'clock okay?"

"That's great. I'll bring my notes."

Smiling, Samantha hung up the phone.

¤ ¤ ¤

After work, Jonathon decided to swing by Mark's house with a copy of the e-mail he received from Dr. Richmond. Mark's son George was visiting when Jonathon arrived.

"Jonathon, you don't look like yourself today. Is everything all right?" Mark asked as he ushered him inside.

"Grace, George, do you mind if I talk to Mark privately in the other room?"

"Sure," Grace said. "Is everything all right with Samantha?"

"She's fine. I just need to talk to Mark about something personal."

Grace and George sped off to the kitchen without further delay. Mark led Jonathon to the sofa, which was located very close to the kitchen entrance.

Jonathon described the seemingly bulletproof plan concocted by the pastor and himself. "Jesus specifically labeled the punishment of sinners as 'aionios kolasis.' Therefore, both the pastor and I were 100 percent confident the *only* meaning must be 'eternal punishment.'"

"Okay. So what happened?"

"This happened," Jonathon muttered as he put a copy of the e-mail in Mark's hand.

Mark read the e-mail:

-- New Message --

Jonathon,
Below is the response I received regarding your translation request. I hope this proves helpful to you.
Kindest Regards,
Donald Richmond, PhD.

-- Forwarded Message --

Don –
This was a piece of cake. I not only found the most common Hellenistic use of each word, but a digital search located the exact phrase "aionios kolasis" within the writings of the famous Hellenistic Greek writer, Philo (20 BC–50 AD). The passage of Philo containing the phrase is preserved in a Greek fragment found in The Parallels of John of Damascus.

The passage containing this phrase has already been authoritatively translated by Charles Duke Yonge, the scholar who wrote the standard translation for *The Parallels of John of Damascus*. Regarding the passage containing "aionios kolasis," Dr. Yonge translated Philo's words as follows:

> It is better absolutely never to make any promise at all than not to assist another willingly, for no blame attaches to the one, but great dislike on the part of those who are less powerful, and intense hatred and **long enduring punishment** from those who are more powerful, is the result of the other line of conduct.

Dr. Yonge translated the phrase "aionios kolasis" as "long enduring punishment." Given the context of Philo's passage, the length of the punishment would be a few years to about a decade.

Below I've copied the most common Hellenistic use of each Greek word from perseus.org. Notice that Dr. Yonge's translation is fully consistent with both the most common Hellenistic use of each word, and the context of Philo's passage.

| Word | Most Common Helenistic Use |
|---|---|
| aionios | lasting for an age |
| kolasis | chastisement, correction, punishment |

Hope this proves helpful.
Charles

-- End of Message --

Jonathon shook the e-mail in front of Mark's face. "Don't you see? The meaning of the phrase 'aionios kolasis' was 'long enduring punishment'—not 'eternal punishment.' The plan not only failed, it backfired! The phrase means the opposite of what the pastor and I were expecting!"

Mark shrugged. "So? Just consider the source, a secular liberal professor. You're not going to start questioning the way the Bible is translated just because of this piece of crap, are you? Jonathon, all the translators of every major Bible translation—NIV, NASB, and the King James—have all translated the phrase in the exact same way: eternal punishment. You aren't going to let one humanistic madman stack up against all the godly men who have translated the Bible, are you?"

Jonathon sighed, exasperated. "It's just that each time I've looked for an answer outside of the church, I get smacked in the face with an unpleasant surprise. It's very unsettling. I don't know how I can talk to the pastor about this e-mail. I don't want him to think I'm starting to doubt our church's beliefs."

Mark smiled. "If you want, I can talk to the pastor on your behalf about this e-mail."

Jonathon thought about it for a moment. "Thanks. That would be great."

On his way home, Jonathon started thinking, "I've never considered the possibility that Jesus's words may have been mistranslated. What if Jesus actually meant long enduring punishment? Is it possible that Jamie will not be in hell forever? Could it be possible I will see my boy one day in the kingdom of God? Dear God, I don't know what to think."

¤ ¤ ¤

The next day, Samantha arrived at the Church of the Apostolic Fathers promptly at two o'clock. She found the pastor's study and knocked on the door.

"Come in," Pastor Jenkins said in a loud voice.

Samantha opened the door and walked over to the pastor's desk. As she extended her right hand, she said, "Hello, I'm Samantha."

"Nice to meet you, Samantha." The pastor shook her hand. "How can I help you?"

Out of respect for the pastor's time, Samantha dove right in. "Do you know if the Septuagint ever uses the Greek word 'aionios' in any of its passages?" She was hoping that didn't sound like a crazy question.

"The Septuagint uses that word 160 times to be exact," the pastor answered immediately.

Samantha wondered how the pastor could possibly know the precise number off the top of his head. After taking pause, she continued.

"Can you show me some passages that I can use to document that this word means eternal? More specifically, I want to document that Jesus unambiguously calls hell a place of 'eternal punishment' when he used the words 'aionios kolasis' to describe it."

The pastor got a strange look on his face.

"Did I say something wrong?" Samantha inquired.

"Did you pretend to be interested in this topic, only to come ridicule our church?" the pastor asked.

Samantha jumped in her seat. "Of course not, I just came here because a link to your Web site popped up on a Google search. And I saw you had your doctorate in language studies from an evangelical college I respect, and—"

"All right," the pastor said. "I'll be very happy to answer your Septuagint question. The short answer is no."

The pastor leaned back in his chair as if to signify that he completely addressed her question.

"I'm sorry. I don't understand. No what?"

The pastor replied with a wry grin. "You asked me if I could help you document that the Septuagint exclusively uses the word aionios to convey the idea of eternity. And the answer is no, I cannot."

Samantha felt dejected. "So you're not willing to help me."

"It's not that, Samantha. It's just that the Septuagint documents that aionios doesn't inherently express the idea of eternity. That's why the answer is no. Here, let me show you a Septuagint passage from the book of Psalms."

Samantha and the pastor read together:

I thought about ancient days; and I remembered the **long enduring years** (Psalms 77:5 Septuagint).

The pastor commented. "The long enduring years were written as 'aionios years' in the Greek Septuagint. Yet here the author of the Psalms wrote that he's remembering aionios years that *are already over*. He's remembering aionios years from the past. If these years have already come and gone, then they certainly can't be eternal, yet the

Septuagint still calls them aionios."

The pastor's grin spread, covering his face from ear to ear. "Let me show you a couple more places where the Greek Septuagint uses the word 'aionios' to describe other things that are already over—other things that cannot possibly be considered eternal."

Samantha read the following passages with the pastor.

> Do not fear that you have been disgraced, nor feel ashamed that you have been berated! You shall **forget your long enduring shame**, and you shall no longer remember the scorn of your widowhood (Isaiah 54:4 Septuagint).

> And they shall build up the **long enduring ruins** that were previously desolate. They shall rise up and revive the ruined cities that were **made desolate for many generations** (Isaiah 61:4 Septuagint).

The pastor said, "That last passage is one of my favorites. Here the Septuagint equates aionios with 'many generations.' That is very far from eternal, wouldn't you say?"

Samantha was getting a headache from trying to wrap her brain around what the pastor was showing her. "But I still don't understand. Why then did Jesus use the phrase 'aionios kolasis' to describe 'eternal punishment'?"

The pastor sighed. "Samantha, Jesus didn't. He never taught that sinners are punished for all eternity."

Samantha's mouth opened wide in amazement. "What are you talking about?"

# Chapter Ten

Samantha sat stunned for a few moments. Pastor Jenkins' words didn't make any sense to her at all. "How can you say Jesus didn't teach that sinners will spend eternity in hell? Isn't that one of the most basic teachings of the New Testament?"

The pastor's voice took on an authoritative tone as he explained. "All theologians used to think the Hellenistic Greek word 'aionios' was synonymous with the English word 'eternal.' That's why, for centuries, it was believed that Jesus taught the idea of eternal punishment. However, in the late 1800s, archaeologists began uncovering many Greek manuscripts from the Hellenistic period[18] that used the word aionios to describe temporary events[19]—including events lasting only a few years."[20]

Samantha nodded as he spoke.

The pastor continued. "As the mountain of evidence continued to pile higher, there has been a growing movement in both the Protestant and Catholic circles to change the way the entire New Testament is translated. The word aionios is used so often in the New Testament that it's fair to say that our entire understanding of the afterlife hinges on translating it correctly."

---

18 "*Beginning in the late nineteenth century, large numbers of Greek papyri dating to the early Christian period were discovered in Egypt.* Some of these contain biblical texts or fragments of Hellenistic literature, but many others are nonliterary: private letters, records of business transactions and civil proceedings, etc. *New Testament scholars soon recognized that this corpus of new material could in many cases illuminate usages in the Greek New Testament for which exact parallels had never been located* in classical Greek literature."—Moulton and Milligan, *Vocabulary of the Greek Testament* (Hedrickson Publishers, 1997), Back Matter. Emphasis added.

19 "Aionios: In general, the word depicts that of which the horizon is not in view, whether the horizon be at an infinite distance ... or whether it lies no farther than the span of a Caesar's life."—Moulton and Milligan, 16. Emphasis added.

20 "*as was Jonathon condemned to* perpetual *[aionios] imprisonment [for three years]*. And now the Romans set fire to the extreme parts of the city, and burnt them down, and entirely demolished its walls."—From Flavius Josephus, *The Wars of the Jews*, Book 6, Section 434, trans. William Whiston. Emphasis added.

A lightbulb went on in Samantha's mind. "So that's why there were so many entries about it when I used Google!" she exclaimed.

"Yes, exactly. And that's why I knew how many times the word was used in the Septuagint," Pastor Jenkins responded. "Because I'm an avid reader of ancient Greek, I had to leave the evangelical community because I could not reconcile what I knew the meaning of that word to be with the Bibles I was told to read."

"What do you mean you *left* the evangelical community? Isn't this an evangelical church?" Samantha asked, frowning.

The pastor calmly replied, "No, Samantha. We don't preach that sinners are cast into an everlasting lake of fire at this church. We preach that the lake of fire is horribly painful—but temporary. It's designed to sear the sins out of the unrepentant soul, to purify and prepare the soul for eternal life with God."

Samantha began to think she was talking to a cult leader. It was time to leave. "Well, thank you for your time. It's been most interesting."

"Are you sure you don't have any other questions?" the pastor asked.

"Oh, I'm sure," Samantha instantly responded.

"We have services here every Sunday. Please think about stopping by," said the pastor.

During Samantha's drive home, she couldn't get the Septuagint's use of aionios out of her mind. She began thinking, "The Septuagint clearly used aionios to describe things that have already ended. And the Bible says that Jamie is going to suffer 'aionios punishment.' Could that possibly mean my son's punishment will someday come to an end?"

"No, I shouldn't think like this," she said out loud. "I shouldn't let a cult leader influence my mind. Shame on me!"

¤ ¤ ¤

That same afternoon, Mark was checking his e-mail when he noticed one from his son George. He opened the e-mail and became furious at what he read.

-- New Message --

Hey, Dad.

I'm sorry, but yesterday Mom and I couldn't help but overhear your conversation with Mr. Webber. I got really curious about what you guys talked about. So I went online and checked it out myself.

I'm really confused by all the stuff floating around on the Web about the Greek word "aionios." Like, I cut and pasted this from one site:

*Written before the New Testament*
> "The second wall is in all other respects like the first but of twice the height. The third circuit is rectangular in plan, and is sixty cubits in height, built of a stone hard and naturally **durable** [aionios]." (Diodorus Siculus, *Library*, book 17, chapter 71 section 5)

*Written the same time period as the New Testament*
> "... as was Jonathon condemned to **perpetual** [aionios] imprisonment **[for three years]**. And now the Romans set fire to the extreme parts of the city, and burnt them down, and entirely demolished its walls." (Flavius Josephus, *The Wars of the Jews*, Book 6, Section 434, as translated by William Whiston)

*Written two hundred years after the New Testament*
> "Here again he means, that Satan occupies the space under Heaven, and that the incorporeal powers are spirits of the air, under his operation. For that his kingdom is **eon enduring** [aionios], **in other words it will cease with the present eon**, hear what he says at the end of the Epistle;" (Saint Chrysostum, *Homily of the Epistle of Saint Paul to the Ephesians*, Homily IV.)

The Web site says that before the New Testament was written, Diodorus used the Greek word aionios to describe something durable— not eternal. And during the same time period that the New Testament was written, Josephus used the word aionios to describe a three year imprisonment—something that lasted far short of eternity. And the website further says that long after the New Testament was written, Chrysostum used the word aionios to emphasize the temporariness of Satan's kingdom— the very opposite of eternalness. So the website concludes that since the Greek word aionios did not inherently mean "eternal" in the time periods before, during, and after the New Testament, then the modern Bible has been translated incorrectly.

Do you think it could be right? Is it possible that our Bibles are translated incorrectly? What do you make of this, Dad?

George

-- End of Message --

Mark was livid. Jonathon's doubts had affected his son. And when he imagined how they could spread to his darling grandchildren, he thought, "I have to cut this thing off right now." He reached over, picked up the phone, and dialed the pastor's residence.

¤ ¤ ¤

Mark went straight to the pastor's house after work and showed Pastor Rick both e-mails: the one from Dr. Richmond and the one from his son George.

"Pastor, this project of Jonathon's hasn't caused the professor to budge one bit," he fumed, "but it's causing doubts to form in Jonathon's mind. And his doubts have already affected my son. This project needs to end—and end right now!"

The pastor winced. "Let me get a handle on this. I'll contact a language professor at seminary and find out what we're all missing. There must be a good explanation for all this. In the meantime, tell George that I'll get an answer to him as soon as I hear back. And I'll also talk to Jonathon about letting go of his determination to change the professor's mind."

"Pastor, I'd like to talk to Jonathon with you, if you don't mind," Mark declared. "I want to let him know how harmful his questioning can be to younger believers, like my son. I don't think he's thought about all the people he could hurt by questioning the word of God."

"Let me get busy finding an answer to all this," Pastor Rick replied. "And yes, of course, we can talk to Jonathon together."

¤ ¤ ¤

A couple days later, Mark received a call from Pastor Rick.

"Hello, Mark. I finally heard from a Christian language expert. He told me that the Greek word aionios had many meanings, with 'eternal' being one of them. And modern translators are confident Jesus used it to mean 'eternal.' They know this from the writings of a fifth-century language scholar named Jerome. For example, when Jerome translated the Bible from Greek into Latin, he translated Jesus's phrase as 'aeternum iusti'—which is Latin for 'eternal punishment.' This leaves no doubt regarding the meaning of Jesus's words and how his words were understood by the early Christians."

"Thank you, Pastor," Mark said with a sigh of relief. "And I hope this teaches Jonathon and George a lesson. I hope they learn not to question so much on their own. Maybe now they'll finally learn to leave these matters to the experts who know what they're talking about."

The moment the conversation ended, Mark dialed George and explained how the translators knew that Jesus's words meant eternal punishment. George said that he felt ashamed of himself. But Mark reminded him that he had done the right thing in talking to his father about it.

¤ ¤ ¤

When the pastor explained his findings—in Mark's presence—it didn't take Jonathon long to understand the significance of Jerome's translating the phrase as "eternal punishment." He felt ashamed for having allowed doubts to enter his mind. The first thing he did was to apologize to Mark. "I'm sorry if I've weakened George's faith in any way."

Mark responded, "George is fine—now. But I think this whole project of yours needs to come to an immediate end."

The pastor chimed in. "I don't think you should have any more contact with that professor."

Jonathon sheepishly agreed.

Pastor Rick put his hand on Jonathon's shoulder as he said, "I've been thinking a lot about all the secular trash you've been exposed to. And I think you need to wash your mind clean of polluted thoughts. So I'm going to give you a scripture prescription."

"What do you have in mind?"

"One of the shortest books in the Bible is Second Peter, which was written by Peter, one of Jesus's twelve disciples. Although it's only three pages long, Peter writes a lot about the apocalyptic end of the world and the eternal destruction of sinners in the fiery wrath of God. I'm going to ask you to read Second Peter once every morning when you wake up and once again every night right before you go to sleep for one full month. As Peter's description of the end times fills your mind, you will understand there isn't even a remote possibility that the souls of sinners will be reconciled to God. All the lies you've been exposed to will give way to the truth found in God's Holy Word."

Jonathon nodded. "Thank you, Pastor," he said. "I'll not only read Second Peter twice a day, but I'll also continue my daily Bible readings."

"You've always been a devout student of God's Word," said Pastor Rick. "And I think that's what has allowed you to stay steady in the faith."

Jonathon began faithfully reading Second Peter morning and night. His life assumed a new calm—until he was blindsided by a new surprise.

Two weeks after Jonathon had promised to read Second Peter, he was completely floored by something he read in his daily Bible reading. Jonathon often read different translations of the Bible to get a variety of perspectives. And he was reading the fourth chapter of the book of Acts in the old Weymouth translation of the Bible. It was the thirteenth sentence that knocked him off his seat:

> As they looked on **Peter and John** so fearlessly outspoken—and also discovered that they **were illiterate persons**, untrained in the schools—they were surprised; and now they recognized them as having been with Jesus. (Acts 4:13 WEY)

"Do I understand this sentence correctly?" Jonathon asked himself as he reread the sentence again and again. "Because if Peter was illiterate, if he was unable to read or write, then how did he write Second Peter, the book of the Bible that I've been reading morning and night? The Weymouth Bible is a very old translation. I need to find out what modern scholars have to say about this."

Jonathon stopped at the Christian bookstore on his way home. He walked over to the Bible Commentary section and thumbed through J. N. D. Kelly's commentary on Second Peter. He was dumbstruck when he read Dr. Kelly's statement that "scarcely anyone nowadays" believes that Peter actually authored Second Peter.[21]

Jonathon thought, "Pastor Rick believes Peter wrote it. And I've always heard he wrote it. But Dr. Kelly is one of the most eminent orthodox biblical scholars. Why does he say Peter didn't write it? And why does he say it so strongly? And if Peter didn't write it, is it a *forgery?*"

Jonathon had no idea that behind that question was the final piece of a puzzle that connected everything he had learned since Jamie died. He had no idea that he was going to discover a conspiracy that has been bitterly affecting Christendom for more than fifteen hundred years.

---

21 J. N. D. Kelly, *A Commentary on the Epistles of Peter and of Jude* (Grand Rapids: Baker Book House, 1989), p. 245.

# Chapter Eleven

On Sunday morning, Samantha decided to attend church with her husband for the first time since the tragic loss of Jamie.

While she was sitting in Sunday school, thinking about all that had happened in the past few weeks, the teacher began her lesson. "This is the last Sunday of Church History Month, and we're going to conclude with a discussion of the Jewish scriptures, the manuscripts that make up the Old Testament section of our Bible. The Old Testament books were written in Hebrew, and the Hebrew manuscripts have been faithfully preserved by the Jews to this very day. Our church was founded on the truth that God has supernaturally preserved his Word in the Hebrew manuscripts of the Old Testament. In fact, in order to become a member of this church, you must avow that the Hebrew Old Testament is the literal inspired word of God."

Samantha began fidgeting in her chair. She knew that Jesus's words agreed with the Greek Septuagint version of the Jewish scriptures, not a Hebrew one. Yet her church required faith that the Hebrew version was the literal inspired word of God.

"The pastor lectured Jonathon about his own doubts just a couple weeks ago," she thought. "So now probably isn't a good time for me to openly question one of the fundamental beliefs of our church. But I still want to understand—when did the church abandon the Greek Septuagint version used by Jesus? And even more importantly, *why* did they abandon it?"

Jonathon noticed the frown on Samantha's face. "Are you okay, honey?" he asked. "Is it too much for you to be here?"

Samantha didn't want to concern her husband with the questions that were parading through her mind. "I'm fine," she assured him.

¤ ¤ ¤

When Sunday school was over, Jonathon caught up with Mark before the morning service.

"I've taken the week off of work," Jonathon began. "Any chance you'd want to get together tomorrow for lunch?"

"Sure," Mark replied. "Anything on your mind?"

"Nothing that can't wait until tomorrow."

¤ ¤ ¤

The next day, Jonathon met Mark at a local restaurant.

"What's on your mind?" Mark asked.

Jonathon stuttered. "Well, I haven't had any more contact with that professor, as I promised you and Pastor Rick. But I came across something on my own that upset me—about the Bible—the other day."

"What is it, Jonathon?"

"You know Second Peter, the book of the Bible that emphasizes the apocalyptic destruction of sinners—the book the pastor recommended I study? Well ... I ... um ..." Jonathon finally blurted out, "Well, according to J. N. D. Kelley's commentary, there is virtually unanimous consensus among biblical scholars that Peter didn't write that book of the Bible."

Mark sighed in relief. "That's it? That's what you're so bothered about? So what if it turns out that another of Jesus's apostles wrote the book? That wouldn't be the first book of the Bible whose actual writer we're uncertain of."

"But in the text of Second Peter the author specifically claims to be Peter, the disciple of Jesus."

Mark was puzzled. "Are you absolutely sure that the author of Second Peter claims to be Peter?"

Jonathon nodded. "I've been reading Second Peter morning and night for two weeks. I know very well what it says."

Mark's puzzlement gave way to absolute certainty. "But the very foundation of evangelical Christianity rests on the truth that the entire

Bible is the inspired word of God! There can't be anything written in the Bible that's incorrect. If Second Peter says it was written by Peter, then Peter must have written it, plain and simple. This Kelley guy must be wrong, not the Bible."

Jonathon pushed back. "Mark, I completely understood why you dismissed the e-mail I showed you the other day so easily. After all, that came from a liberal secular professor. But Dr. Kelley is an orthodox Christian scholar—one of the greatest authorities, in fact. So I can't dismiss his statement quite so readily."

Those words only made Mark angry. "Jonathon, is your faith in the Bible or in people? Are you going to trust God's word or man's word?"

Jonathon was put off by the insinuation. "Of course I will always continue to put my faith in God's word. But who says that Second Peter is God's word? When I read Dr. Kelley's statement, it dawned on me. Jesus never chose the books of the Bible. He didn't name which ones are inspired. Jesus never said that the apocalyptic, fire and brimstone book of Second Peter is God's word." Jonathon was on a roll. "I don't know why it never dawned on me before that *people* chose which books made the list. And by blindly accepting the list of books I was handed, I was blindly putting my faith in the men who chose that list of books!"

Mark's anger steadily grew stronger the more Jonathon talked. "I've heard enough, and I won't stand for any more of this! Nothing good can come out of questioning the Bible. And I will not allow you to try to get me to question it, nor can I permit you to sow the seeds of doubt in my family's minds either. As the spiritual head of my family, I'm wondering whether you should step into my home until you've regained your faith in the truth of the Bible."

Jonathon felt as though a blunt knife had just been thrust into his back. "I guess it's better to end this conversation now," he said, rising to leave.

Mark remained seated. "Yes, this conversation is over."

Jonathon stumbled to the door, left the restaurant, and got into his car. "I'm probably blowing this whole thing out of proportion," he thought. "Dr. Kelley is just one man. And I don't know why I'm listening to one man's opinion without at least researching the topic myself."

Jonathon drove a couple more miles before inspiration hit him. "I know where I can find the answer," he said to himself. He made a U-turn, heading in the opposite direction from his home.

# Chapter Twelve

Samantha couldn't get the previous Sunday school class off her mind. "I wish I could be like most people and just let it go," she thought. "But I can't."

Samantha tried to ignore the contradiction between her knowledge of the Septuagint and the doctrine of her church. But hard as she tried, she couldn't.

"I feel like a hypocrite being a member of the church now that I doubt one of the required statements of faith. I must resolve this—but how? Pastor Rick just recently lectured Jonathon about his doubts, so I can't talk to him. And I don't want to get Jonathon worked up again; he's already been through enough with his own questions. And I don't want to look on the Internet and get confused by another cult leader. Where can I go?"

The answer to Samantha's question came when she brought in the mail. She stumbled across a brochure from the local Catholic university, advertising for enrollment. In it was a directory of numbers for potential students to call, so they could talk directly to a professor teaching in their desired field of study. One of the numbers caught her eye: Father Mahoney—Old Testament studies.

Samantha phoned the priest. "Hello, Father, my name is Samantha Webber, and I was wondering if you would be so kind as to answer a question for me. I was wondering if you could tell me why the Septuagint was initially accepted by the early church and why it was then later abandoned."

"An Old Testament history question—and a brilliant one at that!" Father Mahoney exclaimed. "I wish my students would ask questions like this. Unfortunately, the answer to your question will take a while to properly answer. But I love talking to people who are interested in the history of the Old Testament, whether they are students or not. I grade student papers Mondays, Wednesdays, and Fridays from 2:00 PM to 4:00 PM. Stop by at any of those times, and I'd be happy to discuss it with you."

Samantha's first instinct was to ask if she could call him instead, as she didn't want to impose any further. But she got the feeling that the professor really wanted to talk in person. "I'll be glad to stop by your office."

¤ ¤ ¤

Peter looked at himself in the mirror. He was a skeleton of a man, having dropped fifteen needed pounds. His eyes were framed by deep, dark circles. "I can't search for a job looking like this," he mumbled as he walked over to the cash drawer. "Only one hundred bucks left. And after it's over, so am I."

Peter gazed into the mirror once again, this time looking straight into his own eyes. "What's the point of going on, buddy?" he said, addressing himself. Then he curled his last three fingers and formed the shape of a gun with his thumb and forefinger. He pointed the imaginary gun at his head. "Enjoy your final week," he said to himself, bringing his thumb toward his index finger as if the trigger had been pulled.

¤ ¤ ¤

As Jonathon continued driving, he began to sympathize with Mark's strong reaction. After all, the foundation of their evangelical Christian faith was on the line. He and Mark had both based their lives on the premise that the entire Bible was God's literal inspired word.

Jonathon was desperate to get to the bottom of the issue. He remembered that the local Catholic university library was an excellent resource for historical religious research. So he turned the car toward the campus. Once inside the library, he went straight to the head librarian's desk.

"Can you tell me where I can find some reference works on Second Peter?" Jonathon politely asked her.

"Are you interested in pseudonymous works in general or Second Peter specifically?" the librarian asked.

"Excuse me? What is a 'pseudonymous work' exactly?" Jonathon inquired.

The librarian patiently replied, "A pseudonymous work is one that is written by a person who fictitiously ascribes the authorship of his work to another individual."

Jonathon was taken aback. "Are you saying that someone else wrote Second Peter and fictitiously claimed to be Peter, Jesus's disciple? Are you saying your library considers Second Peter to be a pseudonymous work?"

"Yes," the librarian responded rather matter-of-factly. She opened one of the drawers of her filing cabinet, pulled out a piece of paper, and handed it to Jonathon. The librarian said, "I keep a copy of the *New American Bible*'s introduction to each biblical book. These introductions are sanctioned by the United States Conference of Catholic Bishops." The librarian pointed at the page. "Look at this paragraph here."

> Among modern scholars there is wide agreement that Second Peter is a pseudonymous work, i.e., one written by a later author who attributed it to Peter ... indeed, many think it is the latest work in the New Testament and assign it to the first or even the second quarter of the second century.

After reading the paragraph aloud, the librarian continued. "Since there is 'wide agreement' among biblical scholars that 'Second Peter is a pseudonymous work,' our library categorizes it as such."

Jonathon realized that if Second Peter was truly pseudonymous, then the text of Second Peter could not be inerrant. After all, the text itself says Peter wrote it. "And if the text of Second Peter is not literally correct, then how can I trust any of the other books of the Bible?" he asked himself. There was no way he could easily accept that Second Peter was written by another person.

Jonathon turned to the librarian. "Did the church always consider Second Peter to be pseudonymous?"

"No. It was the modern science of textual criticism that revealed Second Peter to be pseudonymous."

Jonathon had never heard of the science of textual criticism before. "How exactly did this science produce such strong evidence that, as J. N. D. Kelley says, 'scarcely anyone nowadays' believes Second Peter to be authentic?"

The librarian shrugged. "Now you're getting way beyond my area of expertise. Perhaps you should talk to the priest who heads our New Testament studies department."

"Well, I'm not sure how willing he'd be to talk to a stranger off the street about this."

"Nonsense." The librarian smiled. "Most of the professors here are very passionate about their areas of expertise, especially those related to religious issues. There's nothing they like more than to find an eager listener who is genuinely interested in what they have to say!"

Without even asking, the librarian reached for her phone, dialed a number, and listened to the earpiece for a few seconds. "Father Thomas," she said. "This is Sister Catherine Johnson over at the library. I have a member of the community in front of me who wants to understand how Second Peter came to be classified as pseudonymous by biblical scholars. May I send him over?"

¤ ¤ ¤

Samantha finished straightening up the living room and then gazed at the clock on the wall. "It's two o'clock," she thought. "And today is Monday. If I head over to the Catholic university now, I can catch the professor in his office." Samantha scribbled a quick note telling her husband she was going out.

On her way to the office for Old Testament studies, Samantha noticed that the office was precisely across the hall from the office for New Testament studies.

Just as Samantha walked through the opened door of the Old Testament studies, Jonathon turned the corner of the hallway, just missing her. As Jonathon got within two steps of being able to see Samantha in the other office, she closed the door at the professor's request.

¤ ¤ ¤

Father Mahoney motioned for Samantha to take a seat. "You wanted to know why the church abandoned the Septuagint, is that right?"

"Yes, I want to know when and why the church decided to replace it," she replied.

The priest studied Samantha. "Why do you want to know this?"

"Just personal curiosity. I noticed that the quotes from Jesus don't match the Old Testament," Samantha replied.

The priest smiled. "You noticed that. And from your question I assume you already know they do match the Septuagint."

"Yes, precisely," Samantha responded gleefully.

The priest was impressed that Samantha already knew that Jesus quoted from the Septuagint—and she appeared so eager to really understand the answer to her question. As he looked into her innocent eyes, he was aching to tell her the whole story.

Father Mahoney was mindful of his reputation for being a maverick. He often got into trouble for being too radical. He always believed truth was more important than tradition.

"Rather than answer you with the official church-sanctioned version of history, I'm going to tell you what actually happened. I rarely get the opportunity to share what I know. But if you ever ask me to publicly confirm what I'm about to tell you, let me inform you right now, I'll deny it."

Samantha now understood why the priest wanted to meet in person. He had a secret he wanted to get off his chest.

# Chapter Thirteen

Father Mahoney hesitated, then said, "The church didn't choose to get rid of the Septuagint. Rather, a very powerful fifth-century man basically shoved a Hebrew version of the Jewish scriptures down the church's throat, despite fierce opposition from the church leaders of that time."

Samantha was startled by the priest's answer. "What do you mean? How could one man make such an important decision?"

"Have you heard of the Dead Sea Scrolls?" Father Mahoney asked. "The discovery of the scrolls in the 1940s was one of the biggest archaeological finds of the last thousand years—chiefly because they preserved the scriptures used by a Jewish sect dating all the way back to 250 years before Jesus was born."

The priest paused again. "The contents of these writings threatened traditional views of Christianity so much that the church tried to keep many of the documents secret. But despite the church's best efforts to conceal them, their contents were eventually leaked in the early 1990s."[22]

Samantha didn't see a connection between her questions and the history lesson. "But what do the Dead Sea Scrolls have to do with the Septuagint?"

"Everything," he replied. "First of all, the Dead Sea Scrolls revealed that there were different versions of the Jewish scriptures in 250 BC. The idea that there was just one single uniform Hebrew

---

22 "Since the late fifties, about 40% of the Scrolls, mostly fragments from Cave 4, remained unpublished and were unaccessible. It wasn't until 1991, 44 years after the discovery of the first Scroll, after the pressure for publication mounted, that general access was made available to photographs of the Scrolls. In November of 1991 the photos were published by the Biblical Archaeological Society in a nonofficial edition; a computer reconstruction, based on a concordance, was announced; the Huntington Library pledged to open their microfilm files of all the scroll photographs."—From "25 Fascinating Facts about the Discovery at Qumran," (Century One Bookstore, 2005), http://www.centuryone.com/25dssfacts.html. Emphasis added.

version was rendered obsolete."[23]

Samantha had no place to put that information in her mind. Her church had always taught that there was only one version of the Jewish scriptures. And her church also taught that this single Hebrew version was faithfully preserved, via supernatural intervention from God, to this very day. And she was also taught that the Old Testament section of her Bible was translated from this one and only, divinely preserved collection of Jewish scriptures.

"So where did these different versions of the Jewish Scriptures come from?" Samantha asked.

"Great question. As early as 600 BC, the Jewish nation was split apart by invaders, scattering the Jews among various countries. Each Jewish group copied their scriptures in isolation from one another for hundreds of years. For example, the Egyptian Jews maintained their scriptures in isolation from the Babylonian Jews. By 250 BC, a Jewish sect called the Essenes had collected different versions of the Jewish scriptures from different countries. The Dead Sea Scrolls include numerous scriptural manuscripts from the Essenes' collection. The two versions we have the most from are the scriptures from Babylon and the ones from Egypt."

Samantha was trying to follow along. "How different were the two versions of scripture from one another?"

"Actually, there were some very interesting differences. First, in the book of Psalms, the Babylonian scriptures contained 150 Psalms, whereas the Egyptian scriptures had 151 Psalms. Second, the Babylonian scriptures contained a much larger version of the book of Jeremiah. The Egyptian scriptures had a version of Jeremiah that was only seven-eighths the size of the one contained in the Babylonian scriptures. Third, the books of Genesis and Exodus in the Babylonian scriptures say Jacob had exactly *seventy* descendants. However, the

---

23  Note: Different archaeologists use different naming conventions for the various Old Testaments discovered near the Dead Sea. *Archaeologist Frank Moore Cross uses the following convention: Palestinian (the Hebrew texts that match the Samaritan Pentateuch), Babylonian (the Hebrew manuscripts that match the Masoretic text—the text used in modern Old Testaments), and Egyptian (the Hebrew manuscripts that match the Greek Septuagint).* Other archaeologists use other naming conventions (such as pre-Samaritan, proto-Masoretic, and proto-Septuagint). See Vanderkam, *The Meaning of the Dead Sea Scrolls* (pp. 142–144) for more information.

Egyptian scriptures say Jacob had *seventy-five* descendants."

Samantha grew impatient. "I'm sorry, Father, but I've lost track how any of this has to do with the Septuagint."

"Okay, let me cut to the chase. Keep in mind the differences between the Babylonian and Egyptian scriptures as you answer my next few questions, all right?"

"Of course," Samantha said eagerly.

"Great. Okay, how many Psalms are found in your Old Testament—the section of your Bible containing the Jewish scriptures?"

Samantha had brought her Bible with her, in case she needed to discuss her previous research. She looked through her Bible and then said, "One hundred fifty Psalms."

Father Mahoney grinned. "So your Bible has the same number of Psalms as the Babylonian scriptures. I'll tell you right now that the Septuagint has 151 Psalms,[24] the same number as the Egyptian scriptures. Now, look up Genesis 46:27 and Exodus 1:5. And tell me how many descendants your Bible says Jacob had."

Samantha frantically flipped through the pages of her Bible. After finding both Genesis 46:27 and Exodus 1:5 she said, "Both verses say Jacob had seventy descendants."

The smile on Father Mahoney's face grew larger. "So one more time your Bible's Old Testament section matches the Babylonian scriptures. Now let me inform you that the Greek Septuagint says Jacob had seventy-five descendents in both verses, the same as the Egyptian scriptures."[25]

"Interesting," Samantha remarked.

In that moment, Samantha realized the Septuagint was a translation of the Egyptian scriptures, while the Old Testament section

---

24 "*I have already noted that in the Septuagint the book has 151 psalms, not 150 as in the traditional Hebrew text. Psalm 151 has now been found among the scrolls—in Hebrew.*"—From James Vanderkam, *The Dead Sea Scrolls Today* (Grand Rapids, MI: Wm. B. Eerdmans Publishing Company, 1994), 135. Emphasis added.

25 "Exodus 1:5 tells how many of Jacob's descendants came with him to Egypt. For the total the textual witnesses line up as follows:

| Masoretic Text: | 70 descendants |
| *Septuagint:* | *75 descendants* |
| *4QExod$^b$:* | *75 descendants*" |

Vanderkam, *The Dead Sea Scrolls Today*, 127. Emphasis added.

in her Bible was a translation of the Babylonian scriptures.

Father Mahoney observed the knowing look in Samantha's eyes. "I don't suppose it would surprise you now to learn that the Septuagint's book of Jeremiah is one-eighth smaller than the book of Jeremiah contained in your Bible—just like the Egyptian scripture's version of Jeremiah is one-eighth smaller than the one contained in the Babylonian scriptures?"[26]

Samantha smiled back. "I was expecting you to say that. I get the point. Jesus quoted the Septuagint, which was translated from the Egyptian scriptures, while our modern Bibles are translated from the Babylonian scriptures instead," she said proudly. "So you've proven that the Old Testament section in my Bible is translated from a different set of scriptures than the scriptures used by Jesus, the disciples, and the early church. That's amazing! So then why were the Egyptian scriptures—the scripture that matches Jesus's words—abandoned?"

Father Mahoney sighed. "The Septuagint steadily remained the standard Old Testament section of the Christian Bible up until the fifth century. But everything suddenly changed when Jerome, the man tasked with creating a standardized Latin Bible, refused to translate the Old Testament section from the Septuagint. Instead, he insisted on translating the Old Testament section from a Hebrew manuscript that we now know contained the Babylonian scriptures."

"But why did he change it?" Samantha asked.

"Bottom line, Jerome made a mistake," Father Mahoney replied. "He based his decision on some very wrong assumptions. We know this because the Christians were so angry at Jerome's decision[27] that he felt the need to explain himself. So he wrote a book defending his choice

---

26 "I indicated above that *the book of Jeremiah is about one-eighth shorter in the Septuagint than in the Masoretic Text. Among the six copies of Jeremiah recovered from the caves, some manuscripts clearly have the longer, Masoretic form of the text, and one (the second copy in Cave 4) just as clearly has the shorter Greek version.*"—From Vanderkam, *The Dead Sea Scrolls Today*, 128. Emphasis added.

27 "*I beseech you* not to devote your labour to the work of translating into Latin the sacred canonical books, unless you follow the method in which you have translated Job, viz. with the addition of notes, *to let it be seen plainly what differences there are between this version of yours and that of the Septuagint, whose authority is worthy of highest esteem. For my own part, I cannot sufficiently express my wonder that anything should at this date be found in the Hebrew manuscripts which escaped so many translators perfectly acquainted with the language.*"—Letter from Augustine to Jerome (begging Jerome to translate the Old Testament from the Greek Septuagint instead of Jerome's Hebrew manuscript), written in AD 394. Emphasis added.

of translating from his Hebrew manuscript instead of the Septuagint. In his book, Jerome said he noticed huge differences between the Septuagint and the Hebrew manuscript he had.[28] He assumed the reason they were so different was that the Septuagint translators did an incredibly poor job."[29]

"What?" Samantha said in disbelief. "He didn't know about the different versions of the Jewish scriptures?"

"No," Father Mahoney replied. "He did not. And his ignorance of the different versions led him to draw some very wrong conclusions. Jerome accused the Septuagint translators of adding verses, such as the entire 151st Psalm. He also accused them of deleting verses, such as shortening Jeremiah. And where there were wording differences, he claimed they were inept translators.[30] Jerome thought there was only one Hebrew version of the Jewish scriptures. He thought the translators of the Septuagint translated from that 'one and only Hebrew version.' That's why he concluded they did a terrible job. But now that the Dead Sea Scrolls show us there were multiple versions of the Jewish scriptures, including one that matches the Septuagint, we know that Jerome's choice of using manuscripts containing the Babylonian scriptures was simply wrong."

"Wow!" Samantha exclaimed.

The priest continued. "Now, Samantha, it's important to remember that Jerome is not only a saint; he also is a doctor of the Roman Catholic Church—one of the founders of the church's doctrine. Not to mention that the Bible he wrote based on his erroneous assumptions is the standard Roman Catholic text. So I want to remind you that I will never openly state that he was incorrect when he opposed the rest of the church on this matter."

Samantha now understood why the priest refused to publicly back up his comments. He had revealed empirical evidence that a saint

---

28 *Apology Book II,* by Jerome
29 "You must pardon my saying that you seem to me not to understand the matter: *for the former translation is from the Septuagint; and wherever obelisks are placed, they are designed to indicate that the Seventy [translators of the Septuagint] have said more than is found in the Hebrew."*—Letter from Jerome to Augustine, written AD 404. Emphasis added.
30 "it is evident that they [the translators of the Septuagint] were either unacquainted with Hebrew, or have been pleased to say what was not true"—Letter from Jerome to Augustine, written AD 404.

and doctor of the church fiercely defied the church's wisdom for reasons that turned out to be indefensibly wrong. But this wasn't the revelation that shocked her. As a Protestant, she wasn't concerned about the reputation of Catholic saints. She was reeling from the realization that there were multiple versions of the Old Testament.

Her evangelical faith was based on the premise there was only one version of the Jewish scriptures which was supernaturally preserved by God. Now she knew this wasn't true. She now understood that there were multiple versions. And not only that, she now realized that her Bible was translated from a different version than the one Jesus, his disciples, and the original Christian church had used.

Samantha felt the foundation of her faith crumbling beneath her feet.

# Chapter Fourteen

While Samantha was in the Old Testament studies office, Jonathon was directly across the hall.

"Nice to meet you," Father Thomas said as Jonathon took a seat in his office. "I hope you don't mind jumping right in. My next class starts soon, so I'll answer your question as best I can in this short period of time."

"I appreciate any time you can give me, Father."

"So you want to know how biblical scholars discovered that Second Peter was not written by Peter," the priest confirmed.

"Yes," Jonathon replied.

"Let me give you an overview of how this amazing discovery was made. The first glaring problem with Second Peter was that it was not accepted as authentic by any of the Apostolic fathers,[31, 32] the fathers of the church from the first through third centuries."

Jonathon was taken completely by surprise. He had always assumed that all the books in his Bible were the same ones used by the original Christians. "Are you saying that not one single Apostolic father endorsed its authenticity?"

"That is correct. The Apostolic fathers considered First Peter to

---

31  "There is but one epistle of Peter agreed upon, that called his first; and the ancient presbyters used it as unquestioned in their own writings. *We have determined, indeed, that the alleged second is not canonical*"—Eusibius Pamphilus, *History of the Church*, Book III, Chapter 3, Verse 1, as translated by William A. Jurgens in *The Faith of the Early Fathers*, Volume 1 (Liturgical Press), 293. Emphasis added. NOTE: Eusebius was the last of the apostolic fathers. Many evangelical theologians tell their congregants that Eusebius merely considered Second Peter to be a "disputed" book. However, in the quote above, Eusebius states that the "alleged" second work of Peter is "indeed … non-canonical." Eusebius asserted the non-canonicity of Second Peter in unequivocal terms.

32  "In spite of its heavy stress on Petrine authorship, *II Pet is nowhere mentioned in the second century*. The apologists, Irenaeus, Tertullian, Cyprian, Clement of Alexandria, and the Muratorian Canon are completely silent about it. Its first attestation is in Origen, but according to him the letter is contested (αμφιβαλλεται). *Eusebius lists it among the antilegomena … Even down to the fourth century II Pet was largely unknown or not recognized as canonical.*"—From Werner Kummel, *Introduction to the New Testament* (Nashville, TN: Abingdon Press, 1975), 434. Emphasis added.

be authentic. But when Second Peter began circulating, they noticed that its vocabulary, grammar, and style didn't even remotely resemble First Peter.[33] This caused them too much suspicion to endorse Second Peter as being written by the same person."

"But I don't understand: I read that Peter was illiterate," said Jonathon. "So how did he write First Peter?"

"Peter *was* illiterate. He dictated the content of First Peter to an amanuensis, a person hired to put spoken words into writing. A good amanuensis was carefully trained to maintain the speaker's words, grammar, and style."

"All right, that makes sense," Jonathon responded. "But why did the church eventually embrace the authenticity of Second Peter if it was written so differently than First Peter?"

"Here's where the plot thickens," Father Thomas replied. "Jerome, one of the most powerful men of the fifth century, campaigned for Second Peter to be added to the biblical canon[34]—the list of books considered to be authentic and inspired. He speculated that there might be a good reason why the vocabulary, grammar, and style of Second Peter were all radically different than First Peter. Jerome supposed that Peter could have hired an unskilled, poorly educated amanuensis when he dictated Second Peter.[35] And Jerome further imagined this bad amanuensis wrote Second Peter using his own personal words and style instead of dutifully preserving Peter's."

Jonathon couldn't believe his ears. "Wait a minute. Are you telling me that Second Peter was canonized based on the speculative premise that neither Peter nor God chose the words; rather, a bad amanuensis did?"

---

33 "The language and style of 2 Peter is very different from that of 1 Peter. The two works could not have come from the same man."—David Meade, *Pseudonymity and Canon* (Grand Rapids, MI: Wm. B. Eerdmans Publishing Company, 1987), 180.

34 *"the authority of St. Jerome finally brought about the admission of 2 Peter's authenticity.* It was admitted to the *Vulgate*, and the synod convoked by Pope Damasus in 382 expressly attributes it to St. Peter."— "Epistles of Peter," *The Catholic Encyclopedia*, Volume XI, Nihil Obstat, February 1, 1911 (New York: Robert Appleton Company, 1911). Emphasis added.

35 "St. Jerome says: 'the two Epistles attributed to St. Peter differ in style, character, and the construction of the words, which proves that according to the exigencies of the moment St. Peter made use of different interpreters [amanuenses]' (Ep. cxx ad Hedib.)."—"Epistles of Peter," *The Catholic Encyclopedia*, Volume XI, Nihil Obstat, February 1, 1911 (New York: Robert Appleton Company, 1911).

The priest nodded. "Absolutely. In Greek, the words of Second Peter are crude, the grammar is mangled, and the style is atrocious. From a language perspective, Second Peter was written very poorly. Nonetheless, Jerome convinced the church to add Second Peter to its canon based upon his purely speculative 'bad amanuensis' argument."

Jonathon was reeling. "Okay. Now I understand how it finally became part of the Bible's canon. But how was it possible for modern scholars to determine that a bad amanuensis really didn't write it for Peter? How did they discredit Jerome's argument?"

"The most damning evidence came from the field of etymology," the priest explained. "And it's really quite interesting how etymologists sealed the case. Etymologists study how the meanings of words change over time. Take the word 'nice' for example. In medieval times, a very naughty woman with loose morals was referred to as a nice woman. Later, the word became a complimentary term, though still immoral. Eventually the immorality of the word was dropped, and the word became simply complimentary.[36] And now today, a nice child is considered to be a well-behaved child, and a nice person is a decent human being."

"I never knew that!" Jonathon exclaimed.

The priest continued. "In the span of six hundred years, the word 'nice' changed several times and eventually came to mean the opposite of its original definition. It is quite common for words to change meanings. At one point in time, 'brave' meant 'cowardice,' 'girl' referred to 'a young person of either sex,' and 'sophisticated' meant 'corrupted.'"[37]

"Oh, I get it," Jonathon butted in. "Etymologists can determine the general time frame of a document by the way words are used."

The priest nodded. "And not just general time frames. Given enough time-changed words, etymologists can narrow in to a specific time period. For example, let's say that an etymologist came across a

---

36 "The medieval English play *Everyman*, recorded in the late 1400s, describes a woman of questionable virtue as being "nice." *Back then nice meant "having loose morals." In subsequent years, that word was seen as first being complimentary, though still immoral. Eventually the immoral sense was lost. The word was simply complimentary. Now we sing a song at Christmas time that tells us naughty and nice are opposites!"*— *English+ News*, February 2002, http://englishplus.com/news/news0202.htm. Emphasis added.

37 "The Origin of Words and Names," Krysstal.com, http://www.krysstal.com/wordname.html.

manuscript that had the words 'nice,' 'brave,' 'girl,' and 'sophisticated.' The etymologist can determine the general time period of the manuscript by looking at the way any one of these words is used. And by looking at how all the words are used together, he can pinpoint the time period with great precision."

"Okay, Father, that's very interesting. But what does this have to do with Second Peter?" Jonathon asked.

"In the last century, numerous ancient Greek manuscripts have been unearthed, supplying literary scholars with a wealth of information. Etymologists have used the abundance of manuscripts to trace the changes in meaning of ancient Greek words and phrases. And when etymologists read Second Peter in its original Greek, they noticed a huge problem. Second Peter uses words and phrases in ways that didn't exist until the second century. So it's not possible that Second Peter was written by a first-century apostle such as Peter. The language used in Second Peter is not compatible with first-century Greek."

Jonathon was beside himself. Everything the professor said made complete sense.

The priest reached over and took a piece of paper off his desk. "Here, you can keep this. I knew I didn't have much time, so I had this photocopied for you. I've circled the paragraph most pertinent to our discussion."

Jonathon read the circled paragraph:

> The conceptual world and the rhetorical language are so strongly influenced by Hellenism as to rule out Peter definitely, nor could it have been written by one of his helpers or pupils under instructions from Peter. Not even at some time after the death of the apostle. (*Introduction to the New Testament*, Kummel, pp. 430–434.)

"I have to get to my next class," the priest excused himself. "In parting, let me tell you that there are at least half a dozen different proofs that independently point to a second-century authorship of Second Peter[38]—generations after Peter's death. Etymology was just one of them. There isn't an evidence-based scholar who doesn't

---

38 See Kummel, *Introduction to the New Testament*, pp. 430–434.

concede this fact. Jerome made a mistake in considering Peter to be a potential author of Second Peter. But the Holy Church still upholds Second Peter as being an appropriate part of the Bible, since all of its doctrines are sound." The priest looked at his watch. "I have to go now."

¤ ¤ ¤

Jonathon exited the office wondering, "How in the world am I going to tell Samantha?" Just as he finished that thought, he glanced up and found himself standing face-to-face with her. She had just walked out of the office across the hall.

Jonathon stood there, startled for a moment by the unexpected encounter. Then he thought, "Maybe this is a sign from God that I should tell her now." He mustered up his courage and said, "Honey, I know this sounds unbelievable, but I just learned that Second Peter wasn't written by the apostle Peter. It was added to the Bible because of the mistaken ideas of a fifth-century man named Jerome."

Samantha gulped. "Did you say *Jerome*?"

"Yes."

Samantha continued. "Well, I just learned that the entire Old Testament section used in our Bibles is translated from the wrong version of the Jewish scriptures. The original Bible's version of the Jewish scriptures was erroneously discarded by the same man— Jerome."

Jonathon's eyes grew wider. "Didn't the pastor say that the Greek phrase 'aionios kolasis' is translated as 'eternal punishment' because that was how *Jerome* translated it in the Bible he wrote?"

Samantha's face lit up. "Yes, I remember you telling me he said that."

Another lightbulb went on in Jonathon's mind. "And I also remember that the professor tried to tell me something about Jerome right after his debate with Frank, the Christian history professor from seminary."

Samantha felt a pang in her gut. "Jonathon, I think God has been trying to get us to discover something very important. In four different ways, he's guided us to one name—Jerome. Somehow this Jerome fellow has something to do with us and our lives. But what could that possibly be?"

# Chapter Fifteen

On Monday evening, Dr. Richmond poured himself a glass of wine before settling into his lounge chair. He took a sip of the cabernet, then placed the wineglass on the end table. When he saw the beautifully framed picture next to the glass, tears filled his eyes.

He picked the picture up. Bringing it to his lips, he kissed it. "Maggie, I miss you so much."

Magdalene was Dr. Richmond's sister. She had also been his closest friend. The bond between them had grown very strong after she took a faculty position at SU, a job she had accepted just to be closer to her brother. She was a vivacious, fun-loving person who put a smile on the faces of everyone around her.

Maggie had lived with her boyfriend Gary, who refused to marry her even though they had a daughter together. For years she had been fine with their arrangement. But when she started attending a fire-and-brimstone-preaching Pentecostal Church, everything changed. The preacher had convinced her that she and her boyfriend were living in sin. But Maggie couldn't bear the thought of leaving him. So she lived each day racked with guilt.

When Dr. Richmond saw his sister's picture, he recalled the day she entered his office, shaking uncontrollably. "Donny," she cried, "I've just been diagnosed with breast cancer."

Maggie began attending healing services at her church and refused medical treatment as a demonstration of her faith—an action highly recommended by her pastor. After many months of unanswered prayers, she became convinced that God wanted her to have cancer.

Dr. Richmond sat in his lounge chair, staring teary-eyed at the picture. He remembered how hard he had fought to comfort his sister. "Maggie, it's crazy to think that God *wants* you to suffer. You've got to stop torturing yourself."

"But, Donny," she replied, "if God didn't want me to have cancer, he would heal me. God knows I wasn't Christian enough to leave Gary. That's why he's punishing me. Now I will die and go to hell—just like I deserve. It's my own fault." Maggie paused, then started quivering. "Donny, I'm terrified of going to hell."

"Maggie, listen to me," Dr. Richmond begged. "Your religious beliefs are destroying you. The stress is sucking the life out of your body. You have to stop making yourself sicker with all this religious bullcrap."

But Maggie firmly believed in the everlasting lake of fire, and she was convinced that her soul was destined to spend eternity suffering there. Day after day, month after month, Dr. Richmond watched his sister becoming more miserable and more depressed. He felt powerless to help her.

Only eighteen months after the diagnosis, Maggie's frail body lay in the hospital, weak and worn out. Dr. Richmond was sitting next to his sister's bed when she sensed that her death was imminent. Her eyes filled with terror. She started screaming, "Don't let me go!" as she clawed the bedsheets, desperately trying to hold on. Then, all at once, it was over.

Dr. Richmond blamed Maggie's religious indoctrination for shortening her life. But what made him the most furious was the agony it caused her while she was alive.

He looked again at the picture in his hand. "Maggie, I regret that I wasn't able to help you live a happier life. I'm so sorry I didn't know about the Jerome conspiracy while you were still alive."

Then his mind drifted to the time he had tried to tell Jonathon about the conspiracy, at the end of the conference call. "I shouldn't have allowed Jonathon to hang up so quickly. I should have insisted he listen to me. Perhaps I could've spared him and his wife the same terrible pain."

The moment Dr. Richmond started wishing he had talked to Jonathon about Jerome, his cell phone started ringing. The caller ID said "JONATHON WEBBER."

Dr. Richmond wiped the tears from his eyes, took a deep breath to clear his head, and answered his phone. "Jonathon, glad to hear from you again."

Jonathon was relieved the professor sounded so enthusiastic. "Professor—"

"Just call me Don."

"Thanks. I really hate to impose, but the last time we talked, you started telling me about a man named Jerome. And I want to apologize for cutting you off. I'd like to learn everything I can about this man, and I was wondering if you'd be willing to help."

The professor stared at the picture of Magdalene in his hand. "Maggie, are you behind this?" he mused. Then he set the picture down and replied. "It's really too bad that I can't explain everything in person. There is so much you and your wife need to know about Jerome."

Jonathon wondered, "What does God want Samantha and me to know about this fellow from the fifth century? Whatever it is, it must be very important."

As the head of a highly successful engineering firm, Jonathon had the benefit of extra time and money. "I've already decided to take this week off," he said. "I can easily fly out to San Francisco to meet with you in person."

Dr. Richmond was pleasantly surprised by Jonathon's offer. "I think that would be much better, if you really don't mind making the trip."

Jonathon laughed. "You wouldn't believe me if I told you the number of times the name Jerome has popped up in my life since I met you. It seems that every time I ask God to guide me about something, he brings me back to Jerome. I am ready to listen to whatever you have to tell me. And if you think I'd understand better in person, then I'll make that happen. How's Thursday evening?"

"Perfect."

When Jonathon hung up the phone, Samantha was standing next to him.

"I'm coming with you, of course," Samantha told her husband.

Jonathon was surprised to hear that. "Are you sure you're up to it?"

"God is guiding me to the same place as you. We'll figure this out together, just as we always have done." The couple kissed.

The phone rang and spoiled the mood. Jonathon answered it. It was Pastor Rick.

"Jonathon, I'm very concerned about you," the pastor said. "Mark told me you doubt the inerrancy of the Bible. Is this right?"

"Oh no, Pastor. Just one book of the Bible." The words slipped out of Jonathon's mouth. He couldn't believe he'd said that.

"I don't know what's been happening to your faith lately, Jonathon. But I must remind you that you are not only a member of the church; you also sit on the church board. I'm sure I don't need to even say it, but if you don't accept that every book in the Bible is the literal inspired word of God, I cannot have you in any position of authority in the church."

Jonathon was too shocked to continue the conversation. "Pastor, Samantha and I will be going out of town on Thursday. Can we talk about this in your office Saturday afternoon?"

"Sure."

¤ ¤ ¤

On Thursday evening, Peter went to the cash drawer one last time. "Only fifty bucks left," he said to himself, "and tonight it will all be gone."

Peter picked up a picture of Jamie. "Why did you have to be the one who died? At least you had a life. Well, anyway, it won't be long before I join you. One more high; then it'll be lights out for Pete."

Peter threw the picture against the wall, smashing the glass. Then he stuffed the last fifty dollars in his pocket and took his final trip to Star Dust.

¤ ¤ ¤

Dr. Richmond warmly welcomed the Webbers into his San Francisco home.

Jonathon's eyebrows went up in surprise when he noticed that the professor had set up a flip chart in the living room for their meeting. "Don," he said, "while I really appreciate all the trouble you've gone through on our behalf, I have to say I'm surprised."

Dr. Richmond bowed his head. "I have tremendous empathy for your situation. I also suffered a tragic loss in my family when my sister died of cancer. Her final months on earth were spent obsessing over the idea that she was fated to spend eternity trapped in the fires of hell. I did everything I could to comfort her, but she only continued spiraling downward until the bitter end."

"I'm so sorry for your loss," said Samantha.

Dr. Richmond nodded, acknowledging Samantha's condolence. Then he continued. "While Maggie was alive, I began researching the history behind the doctrine of eternal damnation. I wanted to understand how the Christian church ever came to teach such a vile, sinister concept. Sadly, it wasn't until after my sister's death that the pieces of the historical puzzle all came together—revealing a monstrous conspiracy."

"'Conspiracy' is such a strong word," Samantha remarked.

"Yes," the professor replied. "And I choose my words carefully."

As the gravity of the professor's words dawned on Samantha, she was sitting on pins and needles. "So then what is this conspiracy? And what could it possibly have to do with Jonathon and me?"

# Chapter Sixteen

Dr. Richmond explained, "Once I began researching the doctrine of eternal damnation, it didn't take me long to realize there was a great historical mystery that needed to be solved."

"What mystery?" Samantha asked.

"Historical documents from the second century—the *Sybilline Oracles* and *The Apocalypse of Peter*—reveal that the majority of the earliest churches in both the East and the West taught the doctrine of temporary punishment. History also shows that over the next couple centuries six orthodox Christian theological schools were established—with five of them teaching temporary punishment as official biblical doctrine as well. In other words, from the inception of Christianity up until the fifth century, the doctrine of temporary punishment was the mainstream, majority view—the view of most laymen, most churches, and most theological institutions as well. However by the end of the fifth century everything had suddenly and drastically changed. Almost all at once, every new Christian was being taught the doctrine of eternal damnation in hell. So here was the great mystery: what happened in the fifth century that suddenly and dramatically changed the course of the Christian faith?"

"And let me guess," Jonathon interjected, "at the center of it all you found Jerome."

"Precisely," Dr. Richmond affirmed. "A major world change was taking place in the fifth century—the Latin language was beginning to replace Greek as the common shared language. Therefore the pope asked a language scholar named Jerome to create an official church sanctioned Latin version of the Bible, the Latin Vulgate. And here is where history turned on a dime. You see, as I studied Jerome's new Latin Bible (the Latin Vulgate) I came to understand the Christian religion can be divided into two distinct time periods: 'Before Jerome' and 'After Jerome.'"

Without saying another word, Dr. Richmond walked over to the flip chart and wrote out the two time periods.

| Christianity Before Jerome | Christianity After Jerome |
| --- | --- |

Then, pointing to the left half of the chart, Dr. Richmond said, "In the time period before Jerome, Christians took much of their understanding of the destiny of the world and the fate of the unrighteous from the Old Testament section of the Bible, with the book of Isaiah being the most quoted by far. In the original Bible's Greek Old Testament (the Septuagint), the book of Isaiah contains an interesting prophecy about a future 'new heaven and new earth.'

The professor handed the Webbers a paper with the following prophecy written on it:

---

**Isaiah's prophecy of the new heaven and earth**

**For there will be the new heaven and the new earth.** And in no way shall they remember the former things, nor in anyway shall it come upon their heart. But they shall find in it joy and gladness. For behold I make Jerusalem a joy and my people for gladness. And I shall rejoice over Jerusalem and I will be glad over my people. And no longer shall there be heard in her a voice of weeping, nor a voice of crying; **nor in anyway shall there yet be an untimely birth,** nor an old man who does not fill up his time. **For the young man will be a hundred years old and the sinner will be accursed dying at a hundred years old.**

Isaiah 65:17-20 Septuagint (Original Greek Old Testament)

---

Then the professor explained. "The book of Isaiah prophesies about the dawning of a new heaven and earth. In Isaiah's prophecy, there are children being born and sinners living and dying—in other words, Isaiah's depicts the new heaven and earth as a transformation of the current earth and its inhabitants. Before Jerome, the early Christians were taught that Jesus is going to return to establish this transformative new heaven and earth."

Without saying another word, the professor walked over to the flip chart and wrote the following words on the left side of the chart:

> *The Bible only teaches: Jesus is coming back to establish a new heaven and new earth—a transformation of the current earth and its inhabitants.*

Jonathon interrupted. "But the book of Isaiah is still included in the Bible today, so what does any of this have to do with Jerome?"

"Well, are you familiar with a book of the Bible called Second Peter?" the professor asked.

Jonathon's face lit up. "Yes—in fact I came here hoping you would be able to explain Jerome's connection to this book."

"Well," Dr. Richmond replied, "from the first to the fourth centuries, Second Peter was not part of the Christian canon—the list of books considered authentic and inspired. It was Jerome who got the church to put it on the list."

"Yes. I know Jerome exerted tremendous effort campaigning to get Christians to accept the authenticity of Second Peter," said Jonathon. "But what I don't know is *why* he worked so earnestly to canonize it. What was driving him?"

Dr. Richmond smiled. "For one thing, Second Peter rewrites the prophecy of the 'new heaven and new earth.'

The professor handed Samantha and Jonathon another piece of paper.

---

**Second Peter's prophecy about the new heaven and earth**

But by His word **the present heavens and earth are being reserved for fire, kept for the day of judgment and destruction of ungodly men**.... But the day of the Lord will come like a thief, in which **the heavens will pass away with a roar and the elements will be destroyed with intense heat, and the earth and its works will be burned up.**

Since all these things are to be destroyed in this way, what sort of people ought you to be in holy conduct and godliness, looking for and hastening the coming of the day of God, because of which **the heavens will be destroyed by burning, and the elements will melt with intense heat! But according to His promise we are looking for new heavens and a new earth, in which righteousness dwells.**

Second Peter 3:7, 10-13

---

Dr. Richmond explained. "Instead of sinners living until they're a hundred, Second Peter says they are going to be wiped out by an intense fire sent from God so that only the righteous remain. And instead of a transformation of the current heaven and earth, Second Peter says the heavens will pass away and the elements of the earth will be burnt up. In others words, instead of the original Bible's transformation of the earth and its inhabitants, Jerome's new story portrays the fiery destruction of both—quite a dramatic change. And by successfully campaigning to get Second Peter added to the church's canon, Jerome succeeded in getting Christians to accept Second Peter's violent depiction as 'divinely inspired.' Now even to this day, Christians believe the new heaven and earth will be preceded by a fiery apocalypse according to the supposedly inspired words of Second Peter."

The professor then wrote on the right side of the page:

*The Bible now teaches: God is going to disintegrate the earth and annihilate sinners in an intense fire right before Jesus returns to setup a new heaven and new earth wherein only the Christians shall live.*

"While it's interesting that Second Peter opposes Isaiah's depiction of the new heaven and earth, is that the whole 'conspiracy'?"

Jonathon asked, deflated.

The professor calmly responded. "I've only just begun. I have much more to show you. Jerome's efforts go much deeper than that. By the time I complete the chart, I'm confident you'll understand the full significance of the Jerome conspiracy."

Jonathon apologized for jumping the gun.

Dr. Richmond pressed forward. "We have already seen how Jerome got Christians to ignore Isaiah's prophecy, but Jerome had a much bigger issue on his hands—the words of Jesus. In the original Greek Bible, Jesus says that the unrighteous dead will be resurrected to 'aionios kolasis'– temporary punishment."

> *The Bible only teaches: The unrighteous dead are going to be resurrected to face 'aionios kolasis'—temporary punishment.*

Jonathon was surprised. "So, Professor, you already knew what I was up to when I asked you to have the Greek phrase 'aionios kolasis' translated?"

"Yes, I knew," the professor replied with a big smirk. "I played along because I wasn't afraid of how my colleague might translate it. But I have to tell you, you sure showed me how indoctrinated you were by asking me to do that."

Jonathon was a little offended. "What do you mean I was showing my 'indoctrination'?"

Dr. Richmond explained. "Jonathon, on our conference call you learned that virtually every Greek Christian founder believed the punishment of sinners will be temporary. It was pure hubris for you to think—for hundreds of years—that all those native, Greek-speaking Christians somehow missed a sentence where Jesus calls hell 'eternal punishment.' Of course they didn't. Because I knew the early Greek speaking Christians believed in temporal punishment, I wasn't concerned in the least what my colleague was going to reveal. But you summarily dismissed out-of-hand all the Christians who shared the same native language as the book of Matthew, the biblical book that records Jesus's use of that phrase. That was truly amazing to me."

Jonathon looked sheepish. "I get your point."

The professor continued, "And Jerome understood this point as well. He knew most people weren't going to believe in eternal punishment as long as the Bible said Jesus taught something else. But now that he was the sole authority for a new translation of the Bible, he had an opportunity to change it; and change it he did. You see, the Latin equivalent of the Greek word 'aionios' was 'seculorum'. But when it came to Jesus's use of the word 'aionios', Jerome didn't translate it— he changed it. Jerome changed Jesus's use of the word by substituting in the Latin word 'aeternum'—the word from which we derive the English word 'eternal'. So unlike the original Greek Bible which said Jesus taught temporal punishment; Jerome's new Latin Bible said that Jesus taught that the unrighteous will be sent to 'aeternum iusti'— eternal punishment."

The professor then filled in another section on the right:

> *The Bible now teaches: The non-Christian dead are going to be resurrected to face 'aeternum iusti'—eternal punishment.*

A light bulb went off in Samantha's mind. "I've learned that the Septuagint used the Greek word aionios in many places to describe events that have already ended—events that cannot possibly be considered to be eternal. Wouldn't Jerome's discarding the Septuagint help conceal his translation error?"

"Absolutely," Dr. Richmond affirmed. "And it's one of the reasons why this word is still mistranslated in Bibles today. Since modern translators do not recognize that the Bible's authors derived much of their vocabulary from the Septuagint, they blindly follow Jerome's translation of the word instead."

Jonathon was amazed that his wife knew that. He turned in her direction and smiled.

Dr. Richmond continued. "So we've seen how Jerome undid the prophecy written by Isaiah, and we've also seen how Jerome even went so far as to change the words of Jesus. But that wasn't going to be good enough. Jerome still had yet another problem to contend with—a popular prophecy about Sodom and Gomorrah ... Are you familiar with what the Jewish scriptures taught about the cities of Sodom and Gomorrah?"

Samantha answered him. "Almost everyone who attends Sunday school knows that Sodom and Gomorrah were two of the wickedest cities in the history of mankind. And almost every Sunday school student also knows that God rained down fire and brimstone from the heavens, turning those cities and their inhabitants into ashes."

The professor smiled. "Yes, Samantha. But did your Sunday school teacher ever inform you that the Old Testament foretells a time when the inhabitants of Sodom and Gomorrah will be fully restored as they were in the beginning, as if they had never rejected God?"

"What?" Samantha exclaimed. "I've never heard that before."

"Exactly," the professor said, grinning. "And you can thank Jerome for that. You see, in the original Greek Bible's Old Testament, the book of Ezekiel has the following prophecy."

The professor handed Jonathon and Samantha another piece of paper.

---

**Ezekiel's prophecy about Sodom and Gomorrah**

**And I will turn back their rejection, the rejection of Sodom and her daughters**; and I will turn back the rejection of Samaria and her daughters; and I will turn back your rejection in the midst of them; ... **And your sister Sodom and her daughters will be restored just as they were from the beginning.** And Samaria and her daughters will be restored just as they were from the beginning. And you and your daughters will be restored just as you were from the beginning.

Ezekiel 16:53,55 Septuagint (Original Greek Old Testament)

---

Then he explained, "As you can see, in the original Bible, the final fate of even the wickedest inhabitants of the earth is not an eternity in the fires of hell—its total and complete restoration. At some point during the restoration of the earth and its inhabitants, Ezekiel foresaw the total restoration of the greatest sinners on the planet—a restoration so complete it would be as if they had never rejected God in the first place."

Dr. Richmond walked over to the flipchart and wrote the following on the left side:

> *The Bible only teaches: Sometime after their punishment, even the inhabitants of the wicked cities of Sodom and Gomorrah will be fully restored to their original state—as if they had never rejected God in the first place.*

"Wow," Samantha gasped. "I really had no idea something like that is written in the Old Testament!"

"That's because Jerome's counterpunch succeeded."

"What do you mean?"

Dr. Richmond explained. "Jerome knew he couldn't get people to believe in eternal punishment as long as they believed the wicked inhabitants of Sodom and Gomorrah would be fully restored, so he added another book to his Bible; a book that completely rewrote Sodom and Gomorrah's fate. Jerome added a Latin version of the book of Jude—another book of the Bible that was not considered canonical until Jerome.[39] And Jerome's Latin version of Jude has the following statement about Sodom and Gomorrah:"

The professor handed the Webbers another piece of paper.

---

**Jude's statement about Sodom and Gomorrah**

Just as **Sodom and Gomorrha** and the neighbouring cities, in like manner, having given themselves to fornication and going after other flesh, **were made an example, suffering the punishment of eternal fire.**

Jude 1:7 as found in Jerome's Latin Vulgate Bible

---

Then the professor explained. "So instead of Sodom and Gomorrah symbolizing the complete redemption of even the worst

---

39  "*Of the books spoken against,* which are nevertheless familiar to the majority, there are extant the Epistle of James, as it is called; and that of *Jude*; and the second Epistle of Peter"—Eusebius, *Ecclesiastical History*, 3.25.1–7. Emphasis added.

sinners, Jerome's new story has the cities symbolizing the exact opposite—Sodom and Gomorrah serve as an example of the suffering of eternal punishment in fire."

The professor filled in a section on the right:

> *The Bible now teaches: Sodom and Gomorrah are an example of suffering the punishment of eternal fire.*

"So you are saying that Jerome altered the Bible when he made the official Latin version so that he could get people to believe in the doctrine of eternal damnation in hell?" Jonathon asked.

"Jerome changed more than just the Bible," Dr. Richmond replied. "He cut out parts of the writings of the early church fathers as well."

Dr. Richmond paused for a moment and then turned to Jonathon. "Jonathon, do you remember on our conference call that the Baptist seminary professor told you about a third century father named Origen who wrote extensively about universal salvation?"

"Yes," Jonathon replied, nodding his head up and down.

"Well, prior to Jerome, the writings of Origen and many other Church fathers contained numerous references to the teaching of universal salvation," Dr. Richmond said before walking over to the flipchart and writing the following on the left side:

> *The vast majority of church writings teach: All of humanity will eventually be reconciled to God.*

Then the professor continued. "Jerome knew that he could not get many people to believe in eternal punishment while the writings of the early fathers taught something else. But fortunately for Jerome, he was in the perfect position to change these writings as well. You see Jerome and the monastery he established were responsible for translating and copying the writings of the early fathers.[40, 41] And we

---

40 *"Jerome's life at Bethlehem lasted thirty-four years. A monastery was built, of which he was the head."*— Philip Schaff, *Jerome: The Principle Works of Jerome* (New York: Christian Literature Publishing Co., 1892), xvi. Emphasis added.

41 *"The work of the Western copyists begins with St. Jerome (340–420),* who in his solitude of Chalcis and

get an amazing insight as to what Jerome did with teachings he didn't like in a letter written by Jerome himself."

Dr. Richmond handed Jonathon and Samatha another piece of paper.

---

**Letter from Jerome to Theophilus Bishop of Alexandria**

He [John of Jerusalem] charges me with **having translated Origen into Latin**. In this I do not stand alone for the confessor Hilary has done the same, and we are both at one in this that while **we have rendered all that is useful, we have cut away all that was harmful.** Let him read our versions for himself, if he knows how; or else, if he cannot quite take it in, let him use his interpreters and then he will come to know that I deserve nothing but praise for the work on which he grounds a charge against me. **For, while I have always allowed to Origen his great merit as an interpreter and critic of the scriptures, I have invariably denied the truth of his doctrines.**

Jerome, Letter LXXXII, To Theophilus Bishop of Alexandria, paragraph 7

---

"In this letter, Jerome was defending himself against John of Jerusalem who was upset that Jerome had translated Origen's works from Greek into Latin; and even more importantly, he was upset that Jerome cut out the parts of Origen's works that he did not agree with," Dr. Richmond explained. "This letter documents that Jerome not only took a free hand in editing the Bible, he also edited the writings of the early fathers to remove any doctrines that would contradict his new version of the Bible."

"But this letter only documents changes to Origen's writings. What proof do you have that Jerome and the church cut out doctrines from other authors?" Jonathon asked.

"I was ready for that question," Dr. Richmond said with a smile. "Let me show you a very fascinating historical discovery—the second century version of the *Apocalypse of Peter*; a text used in the

---

*later in his monastery of Bethlehem, copied books and commended this exercise as one most becoming to monastic life."*—From Charles George Herbermann, Knights of Columbus Catholic Truth Committee, *The Catholic Encyclopedia* (Encyclopedia Press, 1913). Emphasis added.

earliest churches, written long before Origen was born. The discovery of this document was a particularly enlightening find because when we compare it to a later censored version we can actually see the cutting that took place."

Dr. Richmond handed Jonathon another piece of paper.

---

**The Second Century Apocalypse of Peter**

Then I will give to my called and my elect whomsoever they request of me out of punishment. And will give them a beautiful baptism in salvation from the Ascherousian lake, which said to be in the Elysian field, a share in righteousness with my saints.

As found in Koine Greek in the Rainer Fragment

---

**A later censored version of Apocalypse of Peter**

Then I will give to my elect and righteous the baptism and the salvation for which they have besought me, in the field of Acherousian lake, which is called Elysium. They shall adorned with flowers the portion of the righteous;

As found in a later Ethiopic Version

---

"As you can see, the second century version of the *Apocalypse of Peter* taught that God will pluck sinners from the fires of hell at the request of the Christians, and they will be given a baptism in salvation so they can receive a share in paradise with the saints. It's important to note that this book was written during the first one hundred years of Christianity and it represents the teachings of the earliest churches in the West. While it had been long known that the churches in the East taught universal salvation, the discovery of the second century *Apocalypse of Peter* made two things abundantly clear: the early churches of the West also taught universal salvation, and the church of later centuries cut out this teaching to try to cover that up."

"So the censorship did extend to all the early fathers," Samantha gasped.

"Precisely," Dr. Richmond affirmed. "And after the censorship campaign, the vast majority of writings about the fate of the unrighteous now taught eternal punishment."

Dr. Richmond walked over to the flipchart and wrote the following on the right side:

> *The vast majority of church writings teach: All non-Christians will spend eternity damned to the fires of hell.*

After Dr. Richmond finished writing the sentence on the right side of the flipchart he said, "This sentence completes the chart I wanted to show you."

Dr. Richmond pointed to the entries he had just completed on the flipchart.

| Christianity before Jerome | Christianity after Jerome |
|---|---|
| *The Bible only teaches: Jesus is coming back to establish a new heaven and new earth—a transformation of the current earth and its inhabitants.* | *The Bible now teaches: God is going to disintegrate the earth and annihilate sinners in an intense fire right before Jesus returns to setup a new heaven and new earth wherein only the Christians shall live.* |
| *The Bible only teaches: The unrighteous dead are going to be resurrected to face 'aionios kolasis'—temporary punishment.* | *The Bible now teaches: The non-Christian dead are going to be resurrected to face 'aeternum iusti'—eternal punishment.* |
| *The Bible only teaches: Sometime after their punishment, even the inhabitants of the wicked cities of Sodom and Gomorrah will be fully restored to their original state—as if they had never rejected God in the first place.* | *The Bible now teaches: Sodom and Gomorrah are an example of suffering the punishment of eternal fire.* |
| *The vast majority of church writings teach: All of humanity will eventually be reconciled to God.* | *The vast majority of church writings now teach: All non-Christians will spend eternity damned to the fires of hell.* |

Then the professor stared at the flipchart with a look of satisfaction on his face. "With the entries on the flipchart, we can now solve the great historical mystery of how the Christian faith changed so suddenly and dramatically in the fifth century."

The professor covered up the entries on the right side of the chart, leaving only the entries on the left side exposed. Then pointing to the entries on the left he turned to Samantha and said, "Samantha, imagine you were a fourth century Christian and you have the following situation before you:"

---

**Christianity before Jerome**

*The Bible only teaches: Jesus is coming back to establish a new heaven and new earth—a transformation of the current earth and its inhabitants.*

*The Bible only teaches: The unrighteous dead are going to be resurrected to face 'aionios kolasis'—temporary punishment.*

*The Bible only teaches: Sometime after their punishment, even the inhabitants of the wicked cities of Sodom and Gomorrah will be fully restored to their original state—as if they had never rejected God in the first place.*

*The vast majority of church writings teach: All of humanity will eventually be reconciled to God.*

---

Dr. Richmond gave Samantha time to read all the entries on the left. Then he asked her, "Given the situation presented on the left side of the chart, which doctrine would you believe: eternal damnation or universal salvation?"

Samantha thought for a moment then confidently replied, "I'd almost certainly believe in universal salvation."

Jonathon nodded in agreement.

The professor then covered up the entries on the left side of the flipchart, leaving only the entries on the right side exposed. Then he told Samantha, "Samantha, now imagine you are a fifth century Christian, and you have the following situation before you."

---

**Christianity after Jerome**

*The Bible now teaches: God is going to disintegrate the earth and annihilate sinners in an intense fire right before Jesus returns to setup a new heaven and new earth wherein only the Christians shall live.*

*The Bible now teaches: The non-Christian dead are going to be resurrected to face 'aeternum iusti'—eternal punishment.*

*The Bible now teaches: Sodom and Gomorrah are an example of suffering the punishment of eternal fire.*

*The vast majority of church writings now teach: All non-Christians will spend eternity damned to the fires of hell.*

---

Dr. Richmond gave Samantha time to read all the entries on the right. Then he asked her, "Given the situation on the right side of the chart, which doctrine would you believe: eternal damnation or universal salvation?"

Samantha thought for a moment then replied, "I'd almost certainly believe in eternal damnation."

Jonathon nodded in agreement once again.

Dr. Richmond sighed. "So now you can see for yourself how Christianity changed in the fifth century, and why modern Christians believe what they do—it all traces back to Jerome and his conspiracy. Jerome successfully changed Christianity from a religion of unconditional love tempered by justice to one of dictatorship backed by the cruelest form of vengeance one could possibly imagine."

"This is amazing!" Jonathon exclaimed. "Jerome swapped out the entire Old Testament, redefined the meaning of a key word in the original New Testament, fraudulently added fictitious books, and removed the passages in the writings of the early fathers that were contrary to his ideology. Jerome fabricated his own Bible and his own version of apostolic writings to get people to believe what he wanted."

"Exactly," the professor affirmed. "And when the Protestant Reformation was founded on *sola scriptura*, with the Bible as the only authority, it was founded on Jerome's Bible. Protestantism became a variant of Jerome's religion, not that of Jesus's. Jerome succeeded in hiding the teachings of Jesus and his apostles for fifteen hundred years."

"Unbelievable!" was all Jonathon could say.

"It's very clear to me now that there were two different versions of Christianity: one before Jerome and one after," Samantha said. "But isn't it still possible that this whole mess was created from a series of well-intentioned mistakes, rather than an outright conspiracy?"

"Beautiful question," Dr. Richmond replied. "But I can assure you there is conclusive evidence that Jerome did not commit a series of bungles. The evidence shows that he intentionally misled the Christian community. He knew what he was doing, and he expected to get away with it."

Samantha was more intrigued than ever. "What evidence?" she wondered.

# Chapter Seventeen

That night at the hotel, Samantha could hardly sleep. She was dying to know what evidence Dr. Richmond had to prove Jerome purposefully deceived the Christian community.

The next morning, the Webbers returned to the professor's home.

"Have you ever heard of the Dead Sea Scrolls?" the professor asked.

"Yes," Jonathon replied. "They were a bunch of religious texts, including copies of the Jewish scriptures, dating from hundreds of years before Christ."

"Correct," Dr. Richmond affirmed. "The name refers to the hundreds of scrolls found in eleven different caves near the Dead Sea. Interestingly, only the contents of ten of the caves were made public after they were translated. The contents of one cave—cave number four—were carefully guarded by a strict 'secrecy rule.'"

Jonathon chimed in. "Wasn't there some crazy conspiracy theory claiming that the Vatican was suppressing their publication—or something like that?"

"Yes," the professor confirmed. "Two gentlemen, Baigent and Leigh, wrote a book called *The Dead Sea Scrolls Deception*. In their book, they disclosed a series of letters written by those who had access to the secret manuscripts from cave four. Based on these letters, the authors concluded that there was a cover-up, initiated by the Vatican, to suppress the cave four scrolls. However, in—"

Jonathon cut in. "That book was a national best seller. I read it. That's where I first learned about the Dead Sea Scrolls."

Dr. Richmond continued, "Then you already know that in 1991, a computer programmer got hold of a concordance of the cave four scrolls. The concordance wasn't guarded, because the keepers of the scrolls didn't think it would reveal anything meaningful. The programmer ingeniously fed the concordance's entries into his computer and accurately reconstructed the contents of the cave four scrolls. Then he threatened to publish his findings. The scroll keepers figured the best way to diffuse public interest was for them to publish the scrolls before the computer programmer did. So the cave four scrolls were finally made public."

"And once everyone read the contents of the scrolls from cave four," Jonathon added, "they realized there was nothing earth-shattering in them anyway."

"At least that's what everyone has thought up until now," the professor said with a smile. "You are absolutely right that no one noticed anything 'earth-shattering' in the scrolls from cave four, causing the conspiracy theory to die down. But I have a theory of my own."

"What do you mean?" Jonathon asked.

"I think that in the 1950s, when the cave four scrolls were first discovered, a researcher recognized they posed a huge problem. I believe he figured out that when these scrolls were combined with other church writings, they revealed secrets that threaten the very foundation of modern Christianity. That would explain why the secrecy rule was put in place. But I also think this researcher took his discovery with him to the grave. That's why the modern keepers of the scrolls were not afraid of publishing their contents. After all, they themselves did not know the secret."

"Don, you talk as if you've figured out the Dead Sea Scrolls' secret," Jonathon said.

The professor paused for a moment. "Yes, I discovered the secret behind the cave four scrolls—three secrets to be exact. I accidentally uncovered them when I was reading fifth-century Christian texts during my research after my sister's death. You see, there was not a Dead Sea Scroll conspiracy per se. But when the cave four scrolls are combined with fifth-century Christian writings, they reveal the conspiracy committed by Jerome—what I now call the Jerome conspiracy."

Samantha jumped in. "Was it cave four that revealed there were different versions of the Jewish scriptures: the Babylonian and the Egyptian ones? Was it cave four that proved that Jesus, his disciples, and the original Christians all used the Egyptian scripture and that Jerome's Latin Vulgate wrongly included the Babylonian one?"

Dr. Richmond raised his eyebrows. "How did you know all that?"

Samantha paused before answering. "I heard it from someone who prefers to remain anonymous. But the person who figured out this secret said that Jerome had made a mistake, not that he lied."

"So he didn't find out about the second secret?" Dr. Richmond responded.

"What second secret?" Samantha asked.

Dr. Richmond grinned. "The scrolls from cave four prove that Jerome lied to the Christians in his book *Apology II*, the book he wrote to explain his reasons for trashing the Greek Septuagint."

Samantha couldn't stand it any longer. "Don, please cut to the chase. How could the scrolls in cave four possibly show that Jerome *purposefully* misled the Christians?"

# Chapter Eighteen

Jonathon's cell phone started ringing. Jonathon saw "Mark" on the caller ID. "I'm sorry, but I must take this call."

"Listen, I'm sorry for being so rude the other day," Mark apologized.

Jonathon sighed in relief. "No problem. That's water under the bridge. ... How's Grace doing?"

"She's fine. In fact, she thought it might be nice to stop by your house to check up on Samantha."

"Samantha's not home right now," Jonathon replied nervously.

"Is everything all right with her? Your voice shook for a moment."

Jonathon had never deceived Mark before, and he wasn't about to start now. "Yes, she's fine. She's with me ... in San Francisco."

"Oh!" Mark exclaimed. "I'm so sorry. I didn't realize you had left to get Jamie's things. That must be so hard on the two of you."

Jonathon debated letting Mark assume they were in San Francisco to claim Jamie's belongings. Then he said, "No, that's not why we're here. We came to San Francisco to visit Dr. Richmond, the professor from SU."

"Jonathon!" Mark was almost shouting. "Please tell me you're joking!"

"No, Mark."

"How can you break the promise you made to the pastor and me not to contact that man? Where's your loyalty? I'm sorry I called." Mark slammed the phone down in Jonathon's ears.

The hurt was written on Jonathon's face.

"Are you okay, honey?" Samantha asked.

Jonathon took a moment to regain his composure, then looked

at his wife. "I'll explain everything later. Let's focus on the Jerome conspiracy right now. OK?"

"Okay," Samantha softly replied.

Dr. Richmond picked up the discussion where they had left off. "The only way to fully appreciate the special significance of cave four is to first understand the impact that the scrolls from the other caves had on the world. The vast majority of the scrolls in the other caves contained fragments of the Babylonian scriptures."

"I don't understand why that's so important," Jonathon said.

Dr. Richmond paused, considering how to explain. "Think about this. The Babylonian scripture is the one that's used in current Bibles. So, for forty years, almost every Dead Sea Scroll text published matched the Old Testament used by Christians today. Theologians and academics alike were led to believe that the Dead Sea Scrolls confirmed the integrity of the modern Old Testament."

"That bestseller I read got me interested in the Dead Sea Scrolls," Jonathon interjected, "so I also read a lot of Christian publications about them. And they all said the same thing: the Dead Sea Scrolls confirm that our Bibles contain an accurate copy of the one and only set of Jewish scriptures."

"Precisely," Dr. Richmond concurred. "Prior to the publication of the contents of cave four, that was the general consensus because of the preponderance of Babylonian scrolls. But cave four was different … very different. Cave four contained numerous scrolls from Egypt— scrolls that match the words written in the Septuagint against the modern Bible."

Jonathon balked. "I'm sorry to disagree with you, but I've read a lot about the Dead Sea Scrolls. And everything I've read said that cave four wasn't special. It was just like the other Dead Sea Scroll caves."

The professor addressed Jonathon. "I know it sounds overblown to say it was the contents of cave four specifically that documented the existence of the Egyptian scripture. After all, you are right that the common thinking among scholars is that the contents of cave four didn't reveal anything revolutionary. Knowing that the two of you are engineers, I was sure you would need hard, solid evidence.

So I prepared this handout. It lists all the places where the cave four Egyptian scrolls align with the Septuagint's version of the five books of Moses—the first five books of the Old Testament."

The professor handed the Webbers a copy of the following table:

| Book of Moses | Chapter | Verse | Dead Sea Scroll Reference ID |
|---|---|---|---|
| Genesis | 1 | 9 | 4QGenh1 |
| Genesis | 1 | 9 | 4QGenk |
| Genesis | 1 | 14 | 4QGenk |
| Genesis | 35 | 23 | 4QGen-Exoda |
| Genesis | 41 | 7 | 4QGenc |
| Genesis | 41 | 16 | 4QGenj |
| Genesis | 41 | 24 | 4QGenj |
| Exodus | 1 | 1 | 4QExodb |
| Exodus | 1 | 5 | 4QExodb |
| Exodus | 2 | 3 | 4QExodb |
| Exodus | 2 | 6 | 4QExodb |
| Exodus | 2 | 6 | 4QExodb |
| Exodus | 2 | 11 | 4QExodb |
| Exodus | 2 | 16 | 4QExodb |
| Exodus | 3 | 8 | 4QGen-Exoda |
| Exodus | 3 | 15 | 4QGen-Exoda |
| Exodus | 3 | 16 | 4QExodb |
| Exodus | 3 | 16 | 4QExodb |
| Exodus | 3 | 19 | 4QExodb |
| Exodus | 4 | 6 | 4QGen-Exoda |
| Exodus | 5 | 4 | 4QExodb |
| Exodus | 5 | 8 | 4QGen-Exoda |
| Exodus | 5 | 8 | 4QExodb |
| Exodus | 5 | 9 | 4QExodb |

| | | | |
|---|---|---|---|
| Exodus | 5 | 13 | 4QGen-Exoda |
| Exodus | 7 | 10 | 4QGen-Exodm |
| Exodus | 7 | 10 | 4QGen-Exoda |
| Exodus | 8 | 16 | 4QExodc |
| Exodus | 9 | 6 | 4QpaleoExodm |
| Exodus | 9 | 7 | 4QpaleoExodm |
| Exodus | 9 | 8 | 4QpaleoExodm |
| Exodus | 10 | 15 | 4QExodc |
| Exodus | 10 | 17 | 4QExodc |
| Exodus | 10 | 24 | 4QpaleoExodm |
| Exodus | 12 | 6 | 4QpaleoGen-Exodl |
| Exodus | 12 | 36 | 4QpaleoExodm |
| Exodus | 13 | 3 | 4QExode |
| Exodus | 13 | 5 | 4QExode |
| Exodus | 14 | 10 | 4QExodc |
| Exodus | 17 | 2 | 4QExodc |
| Exodus | 17 | 2 | 4QpaleoExodm |
| Exodus | 17 | 12 | 4QpaleoExodm |
| Exodus | 17 | 12 | 4QExodc |
| Exodus | 18 | 6 | 4QpaleoExodm |
| Exodus | 18 | 13 | 4QpaleoExodm |
| Exodus | 18 | 16 | 4QpaleoExodm |
| Exodus | 18 | 21 | 4QpaleoExodm |
| Exodus | 22 | 5 | 4QpaleoExodm |
| Exodus | 23 | 8 | 4QpaleoGen-Exodl |
| Exodus | 23 | 9 | 4QpaleoGen-Exodl |
| Exodus | 26 | 10 | 4QpaleoExodm |
| Exodus | 26 | 30 | 4QpaleoGen-Exodl |
| Exodus | 32 | 7 | 4QpaleoExodm |
| Exodus | 32 | 13 | 4QpaleoExodm |

| | | | |
|---|---|---|---|
| Exodus | 32 | 27 | 4QpaleoExodm |
| Exodus | 40 | 17 | 4QExod-Levf |
| Exodus | 40 | 22 | 4QExod-Levf |
| Leviticus | 1 | 17 | 4QLevb |
| Leviticus | 2 | 1 | 4QExod-Levf |
| Leviticus | 2 | 8 | 4QLevb |
| Leviticus | 2 | 11 | 4QLevb |
| Leviticus | 3 | 11 | 4QLevb |
| Leviticus | 3 | 11 | pap4QLXXLevb |
| Leviticus | 4 | 4 | pap4QLXXLevb |
| Leviticus | 4 | 7 | pap4QLXXLevb |
| Leviticus | 4 | 27 | pap4QLXXLevb |
| Leviticus | 5 | 6 | pap4QLXXLevb |
| Leviticus | 5 | 9 | pap4QLXXLevb |
| Leviticus | 5 | 19 | pap4QLXXLevb |
| Leviticus | 14 | 51 | 4QLev-Numa |
| Leviticus | 17 | 4 | 4QLevd |
| Leviticus | 17 | 11 | 4QLevd |
| Leviticus | 22 | 5 | 4QLeve |
| Leviticus | 22 | 18 | 4QLevb |
| Leviticus | 22 | 31 | 4QLevb |
| Leviticus | 25 | 46 | 4QLevb |
| Numbers | 3 | 3 | 4QLev-Numa |
| Numbers | 4 | 6 | 4QLXXNum |
| Numbers | 4 | 8 | 4QLXXNum |
| Numbers | 11 | 32 | 4QNumb |
| Numbers | 12 | 6 | 4QNumb |
| Numbers | 13 | 23 | 4QNumb |
| Numbers | 13 | 24 | 4QNumb |
| Numbers | 16 | 1 | 4QNumb |

| Numbers | 16 | 2 | 4QNumb |
|---------|-----|-----|--------|
| Numbers | 16 | 5 | 4QNumb |
| Numbers | 18 | 30 | 4QNumb |
| Numbers | 18 | 31 | 4QNumb |
| Numbers | 19 | 3 | 4QNumb |
| Numbers | 20 | 24 | 4QNumb |
| Numbers | 22 | 9 | 4QNumb |
| Numbers | 22 | 10 | 4QNumb |
| Numbers | 22 | 11 | 4QNumb |
| Numbers | 22 | 13 | 4QNumb |
| Numbers | 22 | 17 | 4QNumb |
| Numbers | 22 | 18 | 4QNumb |
| Numbers | 23 | 3 | 4QNumb |
| Numbers | 24 | 1 | 4QNumb |
| Numbers | 24 | 6 | 4QNumb |
| Numbers | 25 | 16 | 4QNumb |
| Numbers | 26 | 17 | 4QNumb |
| Numbers | 26 | 21 | 4QNumb |
| Numbers | 26 | 23 | 4QNumb |
| Numbers | 26 | 30 | 4QNumb |
| Numbers | 26 | 32 | 4QNumb |
| Numbers | 26 | 33 | 4QNumb |
| Numbers | 26 | 34 | 4QNumb |
| Numbers | 27 | 1 | 4QNumb |
| Numbers | 28 | 14 | 4QNumb |
| Numbers | 30 | 7 | 4QNumb |
| Numbers | 30 | 8 | 4QNumb |
| Numbers | 31 | 30 | 4QNumb |
| Numbers | 31 | 48 | 4QNumb |
| Numbers | 31 | 50 | 4QNumb |

| Numbers | 31 | 52 | 4QNumb |
|---|---|---|---|
| Numbers | 32 | 30 | 4QNumb |
| Numbers | 35 | 5 | 4QNumb |
| Numbers | 35 | 21 | 4QNumb |
| Numbers | 36 | 1 | 4QNumb |
| Deuteronomy | 1 | 39 | 4QDeuth |
| Deuteronomy | 3 | 20 | 4QDeutm |
| Deuteronomy | 3 | 27 | 4QDeutd |
| Deuteronomy | 5 | 1 | 4QDeutj |
| Deuteronomy | 5 | 3 | 4QDeutn |
| Deuteronomy | 5 | 5 | 4QDeutn |
| Deuteronomy | 5 | 8 | 4QDeutn |
| Deuteronomy | 5 | 9 | 4QDeutn |
| Deuteronomy | 5 | 14 | 4QDeutn |
| Deuteronomy | 5 | 15 | 4QDeutn |
| Deuteronomy | 5 | 19 | 4QDeutn |
| Deuteronomy | 5 | 20 | 4QDeutn |
| Deuteronomy | 5 | 21 | 4QDeutn |
| Deuteronomy | 5 | 24 | 4QDeutn |
| Deuteronomy | 5 | 27 | 4QDeutj |
| Deuteronomy | 5 | 29 | 4QDeutk1 |
| Deuteronomy | 7 | 4 | 4QpaleoDeutr |
| Deuteronomy | 7 | 19 | 4QpaleoDeutr |
| Deuteronomy | 7 | 23 | 4QDeute |
| Deuteronomy | 8 | 2 | 4QDeutc |
| Deuteronomy | 8 | 5 | 4QDeutj |
| Deuteronomy | 8 | 7 | 4QDeutf |
| Deuteronomy | 8 | 8 | 4QDeutn |
| Deuteronomy | 8 | 9 | 4QDeutf |
| Deuteronomy | 8 | 9 | 4QDeutn |

| Deuteronomy | 11 | 7 | 4QDeutj |
|---|---|---|---|
| Deuteronomy | 11 | 7 | 4QDeutk1 |
| Deuteronomy | 11 | 8 | 4QDeutk1 |
| Deuteronomy | 11 | 10 | 4QDeutk1 |
| Deuteronomy | 12 | 1 | 4QpaleoDeutr |
| Deuteronomy | 12 | 19 | 4QDeutc |
| Deuteronomy | 13 | 6 | 4QDeutc |
| Deuteronomy | 13 | 18 | 4QpaleoDeutr |
| Deuteronomy | 16 | 8 | 4QDeutc |
| Deuteronomy | 20 | 1 | 4QDeutf |
| Deuteronomy | 20 | 17 | 4QDeutk2 |
| Deuteronomy | 23 | 13 | 4QpaleoDeutr |
| Deuteronomy | 24 | 2 | 4QDeuta |
| Deuteronomy | 24 | 5 | 4QDeuta |
| Deuteronomy | 26 | 19 | 4QDeutc |
| Deuteronomy | 27 | 26 | 4QDeutc |
| Deuteronomy | 30 | 11 | 4QDeutb |
| Deuteronomy | 30 | 14 | 4QDeutb |
| Deuteronomy | 31 | 9 | 4QDeuth |
| Deuteronomy | 31 | 11 | 4QDeutb |
| Deuteronomy | 31 | 16 | 4QDeutc |
| Deuteronomy | 31 | 17 | 4QDeutc |
| Deuteronomy | 31 | 18 | 4QDeutc |
| Deuteronomy | 31 | 19 | 4QDeutc |
| Deuteronomy | 31 | 28 | 4QDeutb |
| Deuteronomy | 32 | 8 | 4QDeutj |
| Deuteronomy | 32 | 37 | 4QDeutq |
| Deuteronomy | 32 | 37 | 4QDeutq |
| Deuteronomy | 32 | 43 | 4QDeutq |
| Deuteronomy | 34 | 6 | 4QDeutl |

Then he explained the table entries.[42] "Scholars have assigned each scroll a unique reference ID. And each ID includes a two-letter code indicating the location where that scroll was found. The letters '4Q' are used for scrolls discovered in cave 4 in Qumran. You will notice that the table I have given you only includes scroll IDs from cave four. You can use this table to test what I've told you about the Egyptian scripture. Simply use the ID to look up the published translation. Then look up the associated book, chapter, and verse in both your Bible and the Septuagint. You will see that every scroll entry in the table aligns more with the Septuagint than your Bible."

Dr. Richmond gave Jonathon and Samantha a moment to digest the profound implications of the table. "From the sheer number of references, you can now see for yourselves that cave four actually is extraordinary. It is revolutionary—provided you know what to look for."

Jonathon was flabbergasted. "But, Don, I'm shocked I've never heard about this. Everything I've read said that the Dead Sea Scrolls only confirm the accuracy of my Bible."

"After the cave four scrolls were published, most Christian organizations simply ignored them," Dr. Richmond said. "They were quite happy with the conclusions they had drawn from the other ten caves. Like an ostrich with his head buried in the sand, they pretended that the 1991 publication of the cave four scrolls hadn't happened. Even to this day, they continue to promote the myth that the Dead Sea Scrolls support the modern Bible. That's why I made this handout for you. Now that you have the truth in your hands, no one can take that truth away from you."

Jonathon's head was spinning. The walls of illusion were crumbling too fast for his mind to keep up.

Samantha's prior exposure to the multiple versions of the Jewish scriptures allowed her to process the new information much more rapidly than her husband. After considering what Dr. Richmond told

---

42 The table entries listing the Dead Sea Scrolls that matched the Septuagint's version of Moses' books were derived from *Notes on the Septuagint*, Appendix A, by R. Grant Jones, as compiled, edited and abridged by G. Tzavelas (2005). Appendix A from *Notes on the Septuagint* was generated using the footnotes in *The Dead Sea Scrolls Bible*, by Abegg, Flint, and Ullrich (HarperCollins, 1999).

her, she reflected back on her conversation with Father Mahoney and another lightbulb went off. "Let me guess. I'll bet it was cave four that contained the Egyptian version of Jeremiah,[43] which is much smaller than the Babylonian one. And I'll bet it was cave four that had a scroll that recorded that Jacob had seventy-five descendents,[44] not seventy as the Babylonian one claimed."

"You're right," Dr. Richmond concurred. "Cave four not only revealed the existence of another version of the Jewish scriptures—the Egyptian version—it also revealed the structural differences between the two. This was a critical finding."

"But Don, I still don't understand how any of this proves that Jerome lied," Samantha declared.

"Okay, let me give you an example. In the Bible, Jesus's disciple John recorded the following teaching of Jesus…"

Dr. Richmond wrote the following on a new page on the flipchart:

*"He who believes in Me, **as the Scripture said, 'Streams of living water shall flow out of his belly.'"—Jesus**[45]*

Then the professor explained. "For five hundred years, this teaching perplexed Christians because they could not find the phrase 'streams of living water shall flow out of his belly' in the Septuagint—their version of the Jewish scriptures. This was a well known problem at the time. So Jerome seized upon this well known problem. In his book *Apology II* he claimed that he had found this missing phrase in the Hebrew scriptural manuscript that he had in his hands, proving that it was superior to the Septuagint.[46] Yet, quite oddly, when Jerome

---

43 "I indicated above that *the book of Jeremiah is about one-eighth shorter in the Septuagint than in the Masoretic [Babylonian] Text. Among the six copies of Jeremiah recovered from the caves*, some manuscripts clearly have the longer, Masoretic [Babylonian] form of the text, and **one (the second copy in Cave 4) just as clearly has the shorter Greek [Septuagint] version."**—Vanderkam, *The Dead Sea Scrolls Today*, 128. Emphasis added.

44 NOTE: 4QExoda is a Dead Sea Scroll fragment of the book of Exodus found in cave four. This fragment records that Jacob had seventy-five descendents. See Vanderkam, The Dead Sea Scrolls Today, 127 for details.

45 "He who believes in Me, *as the Scripture said, 'From his innermost being will flow rivers of living water'"*—John 7:38 (NASB). Emphasis added.

46 "But I was encouraged above all by the authoritative publications of the Evangelists and Apostles, in

translated his Hebrew manuscript into Latin (when he wrote the Latin Vulgate Bible) no one could find the phrase in his Latin Vulgate translation either.

"For centuries," Dr. Richmond went on, "theologians defended Jerome's integrity by speculating that the phrase was indeed in the Hebrew manuscript just as he claimed, but somehow it got 'lost in translation' when Jerome wrote the Latin Vulgate. Without access to Jerome's Hebrew manuscript, no one could prove nor refute the purely speculative defense."

Jonathon was puzzled. "But how can the Dead Sea Scrolls help? They were written long before Jerome."

Dr. Richmond explained. "When the contents of cave four are combined with the scrolls from the other caves, three things became abundantly clear. First, there were at least two versions of the Jewish scriptures: the Egyptian and the Babylonian. Second, the Babylonian version has remained virtually unchanged from 250 BC to this very day. And third, we have all the information we need to identify whether a manuscript comes from the Egyptian scriptures or the Babylonian."

Samantha lit up once again. "Now I get it! Jerome's Latin Vulgate Bible had 150 Psalms—the same as the Babylonian scriptures. Jerome's Latin Vulgate had the longer version of Jeremiah—the same as the Babylonian scriptures. And I bet Jerome's Latin Vulgate Bible says that Jacob had only seventy descendants—the same as the Babylonian scriptures. Therefore we know for sure that Jerome had to have translated the Latin Vulgate from a Hebrew copy of the Babylonian scriptures. Adding the fact that the Hebrew version of the Babylonian scriptures has remained virtually unchanged from 250 BC until today, we can confidently use any Hebrew copy of the Babylonian scriptures to know exactly what Jerome's Hebrew manuscript actually contained.

---

which *we read much taken from the Old Testament which is not found in our [Greek Septuagint] manuscripts. For example,* "Out of Egypt have I called my Son" (Matt. 2.15); "For he shall be called a Nazarene" (Ibid. 23); and "They shall look on him whom they pierced" (John 19.37); and *"Rivers of living water shall flow out of his belly"* (John 7.38); and "Things which eye hath not seen, nor ear heard, nor have entered into the heart of man, which God hath prepared for them that love him" (1 Cor. 2.9), and many other passages which lack their proper context. *Let us ask our opponents then where these things are written, and when they are unable to tell, **let us produce them from the Hebrew.**"—Jerome's Apology, Book II, Nicene and Post Nicene Fathers, Second Series, Vol. 3. Emphasis added.

And therefore we can test not only whether Jerome was correct or not, we can even determine whether he used any deceitful arguments."

Dr. Richmond listened with obvious delight. "You are absolutely correct. And when I realized that, I went through all of Jerome's claims in *Apology II* and compared them to the Hebrew Babylonian scriptures. And I was absolutely stunned at what I found out."

# Chapter Nineteen

Dr. Richmond told the Webbers, "The Hebrew Babylonian scriptures conclusively show that the phrase 'rivers of living water shall flow out of his belly' was never in Jerome's Hebrew manuscript."

"Wow!" Jonathon said. "And of course Jerome had to know that the phrase really wasn't there. So that means—he lied!"

"And this was far from the only untruth," the professor added. "The Hebrew Babylonian scriptures reveal that Jerome's *Apology II* is peppered with deceit. And some of his fictitious claims are quite incredible. For example, Jerome claimed that the Bible's prophetic statement 'He shall be called a Nazarene' was also missing from the Septuagint but was found in his manuscript."[47]

"So what makes that claim more incredible than the first one we talked about?" Samantha asked.

"Because," Dr. Richmond replied, "this phrase was never missing from the Septuagint in the first place! It is found in Judges 13:5."

"Amazing!" Jonathon exclaimed.

"And perhaps the most damning claim in *Apology II* is that Jerome told the Christians that Jesus and his disciples *never* quoted from the Septuagint. Jerome went so far as to state that every Old Testament quotation, without exception, agreed with his Hebrew manuscript against the Septuagint."

---

47 "But I was encouraged above all by the authoritative publications of the Evangelists and Apostles, in which *we read much taken from the Old Testament* **which is not found in our [Greek Septuagint] manuscripts**. For example, "Out of Egypt have I called my Son" (Matt. 2.15); **"For he shall be called a Nazarene"** (Ibid. 23); and "They shall look on him whom they pierced" (John 19.37); and "Rivers of living water shall flow out of his belly" (John 7.38); and "Things which eye hath not seen, nor ear heard, nor have entered into the heart of man, which God hath prepared for them that love him" (1 Cor. 2.9), and many other passages which lack their proper context. *Let us ask our opponents then where these things are written, and when they are unable to tell, let us produce them from the Hebrew."*—*Jerome's Apology*, Book II, Nicene and Post Nicene Fathers, Second Series, Vol. 3. Emphasis added.

Samantha cut in. "I already know that's not true. I've already compared Jesus's quotes of Isaiah to the Septuagint, and I found that they matched the Septuagint against the Babylonian scriptures—the scriptures Jerome was using."

"And I did an even more thorough analysis," Dr. Richmond said. "I compared every place in the Bible where Jesus and his apostles quoted the Jewish scriptures and I compared each quote against the Septuagint and Jerome's manuscript. And I found the following biblical quotes match the words written in the Septuagint while being different from the words written in Jerome's Hebrew manuscript at the same time."

Dr. Richmond gave the Webbers another handout.

### Places in the Bible where a quote from Jesus and his apostles matches the Septuagint and also differs from Jerome's Hebrew manuscript[48]

| |
|---|
| Matthew 1:23a<br>matches the Septuagint's version of Isaiah 7:14 —and not Jerome's |
| Matthew 1:23b<br>matches the Septuagint's version of Isaiah 8:8,10—and not Jerome's |
| Matthew 3:3<br>matches the Septuagint's version of Isaiah 40:3—and not Jerome's |
| Matthew 4:10<br>matches the Septuagint's version of Deuteronomy 6:13—and not Jerome's |
| Matthew 9:13<br>matches the Septuagint's version of Hosea 6:6—and not Jerome's |
| Matthew 12:7<br>matches the Septuagint's version of Hosea 6:6—and not Jerome's |
| Matthew 12:21<br>matches the Septuagint's version of Isaiah 42:4—and not Jerome's |
| Matthew 13:14-15<br>matches the Septuagint's version of Isaiah 6:9-10—and not Jerome's |
| Matthew 15:8-9<br>matches the Septuagint's version of Isaiah 29:13—and not Jerome's |

48 This table is based upon the statistics given in *Notes on the Septuagint*, by R. Grant Jones, as compiled, edited, and abridged by G. Tzavelas (2005).

| |
|---|
| Matthew 21:16<br>matches the Septuagint's version of Psalm 8:2—and not Jerome's |
| Mark 1:3<br>matches the Septuagint's version of Isaiah 40:3—and not Jerome's |
| Mark 4:12<br>matches the Septuagint's version of Isaiah 6:9-10—and not Jerome's |
| Mark 7:6-7<br>matches the Septuagint's version of Isaiah 29:13—and not Jerome's |
| Luke 3:4-6<br>matches the Septuagint's version of Isaiah 40:3-5—and not Jerome's |
| Luke 4:8<br>matches the Septuagint's version of Deuteronomy 6:13—and not Jerome's |
| Luke 4:18-19<br>matches the Septuagint's version of Isaiah 61:1-2—and not Jerome's |
| Luke 4:18<br>matches the Septuagint's version of Isaiah 58:6—and not Jerome's |
| Luke 8:10<br>matches the Septuagint's version of Isaiah 6:9—and not Jerome's |
| John 1:23<br>matches the Septuagint's version of Isaiah 40:3—and not Jerome's |
| John 6:31<br>matches the Septuagint's version of Psalm 78:24—and not Jerome's |
| John 12:38<br>matches the Septuagint's version of Isaiah 53:1—and not Jerome's |
| John 12:40<br>matches the Septuagint's version of Isaiah 6:10—and not Jerome's |
| Acts 2:17-21<br>matches the Septuagint's version of Joel 2:28-32—and not Jerome's |
| Acts 2:25-28<br>matches the Septuagint's version of Psalm 16:8-11—and not Jerome's |
| Acts 4:25-26<br>matches the Septuagint's version of Psalm 2:1-2—and not Jerome's |
| Acts 7:27-28<br>matches the Septuagint's version of Exodus 2:14—and not Jerome's |
| Acts 7:42-43<br>matches the Septuagint's version of Amos 5:25-27—and not Jerome's |
| Acts 8:32-33<br>matches the Septuagint's version of Isaiah 53:7-8—and not Jerome's |

| |
|---|
| Acts 13:34<br>matches the Septuagint's version of Isaiah 55:3—and not Jerome's |
| Acts 13:35<br>matches the Septuagint's version of Psalm 16:10—and not Jerome's |
| Acts 13:41<br>matches the Septuagint's version of Habakkuk 1:5—and not Jerome's |
| Acts 15:16-17<br>matches the Septuagint's version of Amos 9:11-12—and not Jerome's |
| Acts 28:26-27<br>matches the Septuagint's version of Isaiah 6:9-10—and not Jerome's |
| Romans 2:24<br>matches the Septuagint's version of Isaiah 52:5—and not Jerome's |
| Romans 3:4<br>matches the Septuagint's version of Psalm 51:4—and not Jerome's |
| Romans 3:10-12<br>matches the Septuagint's version of Psalm 14:1-3—and not Jerome's |
| Romans 3:10-12<br>matches the Septuagint's version of Psalm 53:1-3—and not Jerome's |
| Romans 3:13a<br>matches the Septuagint's version of Psalm 5:9—and not Jerome's |
| Romans 3:13b<br>matches the Septuagint's version of Psalm 140:3—and not Jerome's |
| Romans 3:14<br>matches the Septuagint's version of Psalm 10:7—and not Jerome's |
| Romans 9:17<br>matches the Septuagint's version of Exodus 9:16—and not Jerome's |
| Romans 9:25<br>matches the Septuagint's version of Hosea 2:23—and not Jerome's |
| Romans 9:27-28<br>matches the Septuagint's version of Isaiah 10:22-23- and not Jerome's |
| Romans 9:29<br>matches the Septuagint's version of Isaiah 1:9—and not Jerome's |
| Romans 9:33<br>matches the Septuagint's version of Isaiah 9:33—and not Jerome's |
| Romans 10:11<br>matches the Septuagint's version of Isaiah 28:16—and not Jerome's |
| Romans 10:16<br>matches the Septuagint's version of Isaiah 53:1—and not Jerome's |

| |
|---|
| Romans 10:18<br>matches the Septuagint's version of Psalm 19:4—and not Jerome's |
| Romans 10:20<br>matches the Septuagint's version of Isaiah 65:1—and not Jerome's |
| Romans 10:21<br>matches the Septuagint's version of Isaiah 65:2—and not Jerome's |
| Romans 11:9-10<br>matches the Septuagint's version of Psalm 69:22-23– and not Jerome's |
| Romans 11:26-27<br>matches the Septuagint's version of Isaiah 59:20-21– and not Jerome's |
| Romans 11:27b<br>matches the Septuagint's version of Isaiah 27:9—and not Jerome's |
| Romans 11:34<br>matches the Septuagint's version of Isaiah 40:13—and not Jerome's |
| Romans 12:20<br>matches the Septuagint's version of Proverbs 25:21-22—and not Jerome's |
| Romans 14:11b<br>matches the Septuagint's version of Isaiah 45:23—and not Jerome's |
| Romans 15:12<br>matches the Septuagint's version of Isaiah 11:10—and not Jerome's |
| Romans 15:21<br>matches the Septuagint's version of Isaiah 52:15—and not Jerome's |
| 1 Corinthians 1:19<br>matches the Septuagint's version of Isaiah 29:14—and not Jerome's |
| 1 Corinthians 2:16<br>matches the Septuagint's version of Isaiah 40:13—and not Jerome's |
| 1 Corinthians 5:13<br>matches the Septuagint's version of Deuteronomy 17:7– and not Jerome's |
| 1 Corinthians 15:55<br>matches the Septuagint's version of Hosea 13:14—and not Jerome's |
| 2 Corinthians 4:13<br>matches the Septuagint's version of Psalm 116:10—and not Jerome's |
| 2 Corinthians 6:2<br>matches the Septuagint's version of Isaiah 49:8—and not Jerome's |
| Galatians 3:10<br>matches the Septuagint's version of Deuteronomy 27:26– and not Jerome's |
| Galatians 3:13<br>matches the Septuagint's version of Deuteronomy 21:23– and not Jerome's |

| |
|---|
| Galatians 3:16<br>matches the Septuagint's version of Genesis 12:7—and not Jerome's |
| Galatians 4:27<br>matches the Septuagint's version of Isaiah 54:1—and not Jerome's |
| Ephesians 4:26<br>matches the Septuagint's version of Psalm 4:4—and not Jerome's |
| 2 Timothy 2:19<br>matches the Septuagint's version of Numbers 16:5—and not Jerome's |
| Hebrews 1:6<br>matches the Septuagint's version of Deuteronomy 32:43– and not Jerome's |
| Hebrews 1:7<br>matches the Septuagint's version of Psalm 104:4—and not Jerome's |
| Hebrews 1:10-12<br>matches the Septuagint's version of Psalm 102:25-27– and not Jerome's |
| Hebrews 2:6-8<br>matches the Septuagint's version of Psalm 8:4-6—and not Jerome's |
| Hebrews 2:12<br>matches the Septuagint's version of Psalm 22:22—and not Jerome's |
| Hebrews 2:13a<br>matches the Septuagint's version of Isaiah 8:17—and not Jerome's |
| Hebrews 3:7-11<br>matches the Septuagint's version of Psalm 95:7-11—and not Jerome's |
| Hebrews 3:15<br>matches the Septuagint's version of Psalm 95:7-8—and not Jerome's |
| Hebrews 4:7<br>matches the Septuagint's version of Psalm 95:7-8—and not Jerome's |
| Hebrews 8:8-12<br>matches the Septuagint's version of Jeremiah 31:31-34– and not Jerome's |
| Hebrews 10:5-7<br>matches the Septuagint's version of Psalm 40:6-8—and not Jerome's |
| Hebrews 10:16-17<br>matches the Septuagint's version of Jeremiah 31:33-34– and not Jerome's |
| Hebrews 10:37-38<br>matches the Septuagint's version of Habakkuk 2:3-4—and not Jerome's |
| Hebrews 11:5<br>matches the Septuagint's version of Genesis 5:24—and not Jerome's |
| Hebrews 11:21<br>matches the Septuagint's version of Genesis 47:31– and not Jerome's |

| Hebrews 12:5-6 matches the Septuagint's version of Proverbs 3:11-12– and not Jerome's |
| --- |
| Hebrews 12:26 matches the Septuagint's version of Haggai 2:6—and not Jerome's |
| Hebrews 13:6 matches the Septuagint's version of Psalm 118:6—and not Jerome's |
| James 4:6 matches the Septuagint's version of Proverbs 3:34—and not Jerome's |
| 1 Peter 1:24-25 matches the Septuagint's version of Isaiah 40:6-8—and not Jerome's |
| 1 Peter 2:6 matches the Septuagint's version of Isaiah 28:16—and not Jerome's |
| 1 Peter 2:9b matches the Septuagint's version of Exodus 19:6—and not Jerome's |
| 1 Peter 2:9c matches the Septuagint's version of Isaiah 43:21—and not Jerome's |
| 1 Peter 2:22 matches the Septuagint's version of Isaiah 53:9—and not Jerome's |
| 1 Peter 4:18 matches the Septuagint's version of Proverbs 11:31—and not Jerome's |
| 1 Peter 5:5 matches the Septuagint's version of Proverbs 3:34—and not Jerome's |

Jonathon was floored. "Of course Jerome couldn't have missed all of these places where quotes from Jesus and his disciples match the Septuagint and not his manuscript. I must admit it; he intentionally deceived the Christian community."

"Okay, Don," Samantha said, "you've also convinced me that Jerome didn't simply make a mistake. What else can I think about a man who published a book filled with blatant untruths to defend replacing the entire Old Testament, censored significant parts of the early church writings, and vigorously campaigned to add Second Peter and Jude to the Bible based entirely on speculative reasoning? The only conclusion I can draw is that he was masterminding a larger plan of his own devising. I think your terming it a 'conspiracy' is perfectly accurate."

"But why?" Jonathon asked. "Why did he do it? Why did he

go through so much effort to change the Bible and the writings of the apostolic fathers?"

"At the turn of the fifth century, the Roman theological school had an enormous crisis on its hands," Dr. Richmond answered. "The majority of Christendom was rejecting the Roman view of God. Mainstream apostolic Christians believed in a God who chose to reconcile everyone, including his enemies, through the sacrifice of Jesus on the cross. But the Roman Church taught about a different God. It touted a God who chose to extend a temporary, one-shot opportunity for being reconciled. And people who didn't accept his provision during their lives on earth would be sentenced to an eternity of pain and suffering. Jerome was upset that the Roman theology was rejected by most Christians. So he masterminded a plan to trick the rest of Christianity into believing in the Roman God."

Samantha interrupted. "But how did the church in Rome come to believe in doctrines that were so different from the rest of Christianity in the first place?"

"The Roman Church did not base its doctrine on either the Old Testament Jewish scriptures or the writings of Jesus's apostles."

"What?" Jonathon gasped.

"The doctrine of eternal punishment is not fundamentally part of the Jewish scriptures," Dr. Richmond explained. "This teaching was introduced to the Jewish community around 150 BC in an apocalyptic text called *The Book of Enoch*. This book paints God as a being who inflicts everlasting punishment on everyone who does not live righteously. The early founders of Roman theology (Tatian, Irenaeus, Justin Martyr, Athenagoras, and Tertullian) all believed *The Book of Enoch* was the literal inspired word of God.[49] And so they interpreted Jesus's words based on its teachings. In essence, this text served as the basis of the Roman doctrine, whereas the rest of Christendom was founded on faith in the apostolic Bible."

Jonathon jumped in. "But if this book was considered so

---

49 "The early Christian father Tertullian wrote c. 200 that *The Book of Enoch* had been rejected by the Jews because it contained prophecies pertaining to Christ. The Greek language text was known to, and quoted by nearly all, Church Fathers. *A number of the Church Fathers thought it to be an inspired work*"—From "Book of Enoch," Reference.com. Emphasis added.

important to the Roman Church, why didn't they include it in their Bible?"

Dr. Richmond laughed. "Jerome did include it in his Bible, but in a very sneaky way. Jerome added Second Peter and Jude, books that recapitulate the major teachings of *The Book of Enoch*. In fact, Jude even quotes it directly."

Dr. Richmond gave Jonathon and Samantha another handout.

| Jude 1:14–15 | Book of Enoch 1:9 |
|---|---|
| Behold, the Lord came with ten thousands of his holy ones, | And behold! He cometh with ten thousands of his holy ones |
| to execute judgment upon all, | To execute judgment upon all, |
| and to convict all the ungodly of all their works of ungodliness which they have ungodly wrought, | and to destroy all the ungodly; and to convict all flesh of all the works of their ungodliness which they have ungodly committed, |
| and of all the hard things which ungodly sinners have spoken against him. | and of all the hard things which ungodly sinners have spoken against him. |

After taking a moment to think about the handout, Jonathon remarked, "But this doesn't mean anything. The Bible quotes from many nonbiblical books. Just because a biblical author quotes from a book doesn't mean they considered that other book to be inspired."

"I'm fully aware that the Bible quotes many other books," Dr. Richmond replied. "But the quote from Jude is different from all the others because the way the author of Jude introduces the quote."

Dr. Richmond handed Jonathon and Samantha a Bible, and pointed to the passage in the book of Jude where the quote from *The Book of Enoch* is found.

It was also about these men that **Enoch, in the seventh generation from Adam, prophesied, saying,** "Behold, the Lord came with many thousands of His holy ones, to execute judgment upon all, and to convict all the ungodly of all their ungodly deeds which they have done in an ungodly way, and of all the harsh things which ungodly sinners have spoken against Him."—Jude 1:14-15

Then the professor explained. "The author of Jude doesn't simply quote from *The Book of Enoch*; the author of Jude attributes those words directly to the prophet Enoch who lived in the seventh generation of mankind. And it is this attribution that is in error. You see, during the second century, it was commonly believed that *The Book of Enoch* was written by the prophet Enoch himself during the seventh generation of man. The author of Jude, and the founding fathers of Roman theology, believed this myth. The author of Jude didn't know that *The Book of Enoch* was written pseudonymously by a fictitious author around 150 BC. So the author of Jude didn't do anything 'wrong' by quoting *The Book of Enoch*, but he certainly was incorrect to attribute the words in that book to the prophet Enoch in the seventh generation of mankind."

Samantha looked bewildered. "But Don, what puzzles me is how did you possibly know to prepare this handout about *The Book of Enoch* in advance, before I even asked my question?"

Dr. Richmond chuckled. "I had already prepared this handout to document the third and final secret from cave four. You see, Jude and Second Peter are filled with references to Enochian doctrines—doctrines about the violent end of the world and the eternal punishment of the wicked. For centuries, theologians explained the similarities by claiming that *The Book of Enoch* was written *after* Second Peter and Jude. In other words, they claimed that the circulating copies of *The Book of Enoch* quoted Jude, not the other way around. But, once again, the contents of cave four changed everything."

The professor gave the Webbers another handout.

| Cave Four Scrolls of the Book of Enoch |
|:---:|
| 4QEna |
| 4QEnb |
| 4QEnc |
| 4QEnd |
| 4QEne |
| 4QEnf |
| 4QEng |
| 4QEnastra |
| 4QEnastrb |
| 4QEnastrc |
| 4QEnastrd |

"Cave four contained eleven copies of the parts of *The Book of Enoch* that Second Peter and Jude are based upon,[50] proving that this book was written centuries before Second Peter and Jude. Therefore, the cave four scrolls show that the theology of Second Peter and Jude is based on *The Book of Enoch*, not the other way around. Or, said another way, cave four documents that the Roman theology was based on *The Book of Enoch*."

Samantha wanted to see whether she understood everything correctly. "So in essence, the Jerome conspiracy reshaped the Bible and the writings of the apostolic fathers to conform to the apocalyptic teachings of *The Book of Enoch*. And Christianity has, since the fifth century onward, viewed the destiny of the world and the fate of the unrighteous based on Enochian theology instead of the teachings of Jesus and his disciples."

"Yes!" Dr. Richmond exclaimed.

Jonathon shook his head. "But there's still one thing that bothers me. I've read the Bible cover to cover many times over the last thirty years, and each time I read it, it feels like the whole book is based on a violent apocalyptic eternal judgment."

---

50 The table listing for cave four Enoch Scrolls is based upon the table of contents in *The Dead Sea Scrolls Translated: The Qumran Texts in English*, by Martinez, Florentino Garcia (Grand Rapids, MI: Wm. Eerdmans Publishing Company, 1996).

Dr. Richmond looked mischievous as he said, "Have you ever seen a magic show, where a magician suddenly makes an elephant appear on stage, seemingly out of nowhere?"

Samantha and Jonathon nodded.

"Of course the elephant was on the stage the entire time. But the magician was able to keep you from seeing it through the clever use of smoke and mirrors. And so it is with the Jerome conspiracy. Because of the way Jerome rewrote the Bible, people can't see the elephant right in front of their faces. They can read the Bible cover to cover and mentally jump right over the numerous references to universal salvation, even though the references are right there in front of their eyes. And because they jump over those references, they feel like the Bible promotes an apocalyptic God whose wrath will be felt for all eternity."

"I don't understand," Samantha replied.

Dr. Richmond turned in her direction. "You have read the book of Ezekiel before, right?"

"Yes."

"And yet you didn't recall the prophecy about Sodom and Gomorrah being fully restored. Why is that?" Dr. Richmond asked her.

"I guess when I read that passage I somehow missed it."

Dr. Richmond nodded his head up and down. "And you have read the book of Isaiah before, right?"

"Yes."

"And yet you didn't question why it says that sinners will be living and dying in the new heaven and new earth?"

"Well, I guess I must have missed that somehow as well."

Dr. Richmond nodded again. "And do you recall that the book of Matthew teaches that people get out of hell 'after they pay the last penny'?"

"I don't recall that...even though I have read the book of Matthew many times."

"I'm not surprised. One more time, you've mentally jumped over a reference to universal salvation. And this is all the result of the

Jerome conspiracy." Dr. Richmond explained.

"But why does it work this way?" Jonathon asked.

"Human nature," Dr. Richmond replied. "Once you already believe Sodom and Gomorrah are examples of eternal punishment, it's only natural to mentally ignore Ezekiel's statement to the contrary. Once you've already accepted the apocalyptic version of the new heaven and new earth, it's only natural to ignore Isaiah's statement to the contrary. And once you're already convinced that Jesus spoke of 'eternal fire' and 'eternal punishment', it's only natural to mentally jump over Jesus's statement that people do indeed get out of hell after they pay the last penny."

Jonathon lit up. "So that's why you call the Jerome conspiracy a campaign of smoke and mirrors. The things Jerome added to the Bible blinds us from seeing what the original Bible taught in the first place."

"Precisely," Dr. Richmond affirmed. "And now that our time is short, I'm going to give you a homework assignment that will blow away the smoke and smash the mirrors, so you can clearly see the teachings of the original Bible with your own eyes."

# Chapter Twenty

Dr. Richmond started explaining the Webbers' homework assignment. "First, I need to inform you that during the second century, there weren't just two theories on the ultimate fate of sinners. There were three."

Dr. Richmond handed the Webbers a piece of paper containing a chart of the three theories:

|  | Final State of the Universe | Method of Getting There |
|---|---|---|
| Eternal Torment | *Heaven and Hell*: The tiny kingdom of God consists of relatively few souls. And outside of it there is an enormous, raging inferno, perpetually torturing the vast majority of humans who ever lived. | *Everlasting Torture*: Sinners are made immortal, then forced to spend eternity in a lake of fire. |
| Annihilation | *God all in all*: The entire universe is in perfect harmony with God. God's presence permeates the universe, so God is all in all. | *Annihilation*: Sinners are extinguished out of existence so that only righteousness remains. |
| Universal Salvation | *God all in all*: The entire universe is in perfect harmony with God. God's presence permeates the universe, so God is all in all. | *Purification*: Sinners are punished, then purified in the fires of Gehenna. After purification, their souls rise to the kingdom of God. After the last soul is purified, the fire has no more material to burn, so it self-extinguishes, leaving only perfection remaining in the universe. |

After the Webbers had read the description of the three theories, Dr. Richmond said, "This chart I handed you summarizes the three theories based on the 'final state of the universe' and the 'method of getting there'. You can use this chart to read Paul's writings in a way that will break the illusion that Jerome created. Through the lens of the 'final state of the universe', you will blow away Jerome's smoke, and through the lens of the 'method of getting there', you will shatter his mirrors. Then you will see the elephant the magician was hiding from you."

"I'm not sure I'm following you," Samantha remarked.

The professor detailed the homework assignment. "I want you to read each of Paul's writings contained in the Bible twice. The first time, I want you to write down each place where Paul states that the 'final state of the universe' is going to be one of perfect harmony, where God is all in all. Then the second time, I want you to go back to each of those places and write down God's 'method of getting there' as stated by Paul. Then, looking back at the chart of the three theories, I want you to record whether each 'final state of the universe' and the 'method of getting there' best fits: the doctrine of eternal torment, the doctrine of annihilation, or the doctrine of universal salvation."

¤ ¤ ¤

During the plane trip home, Jonathon took out his Bible, a piece of paper, and a pen from his briefcase. He completed the homework assignment the professor had given him. He read each book of the Bible written by Paul, looking for "the final state of the universe" and "the method used to get there." He made a little table of what he found:

| Book of Paul | Final State of the Universe | Method of Getting There | Doctrine Being Taught |
|---|---|---|---|
| First Corinthians Chapter 15 | *God all in all*: God is all in all (verse 28) | *Purification*: Christ first gets God's enemies to submit to his authority; then Christ submits to the authority of the Father (verses 25–28). | Universal Salvation |
| Romans Chapter 11 | *God all in all*: From Him and through Him and to Him are all things (verse 36). | *Purification*: God has bound all men to disobedience so he might have mercy on them all (verse 32). | Universal Salvation |
| Colossians Chapter 1 | *God all in all*: all things created through Him and for Him (verse 16). God has chosen to reconcile everything he ever created through Christ (verse 20). | *Purification*: Every being made is created through Him and for Him: all beings on heaven and earth; visible and invisible (verse 16), all beings in heaven and earth are being reconciled through Christ's sacrifice (verse 20). | Universal Salvation |

| Ephesians Chapter 1 | *God all in all*:<br><br>Christ is described as the fullness of "Him who fills all in all" (verse 23). | *Purification*:<br><br>God has put all things under the authority of Christ (verse 22) | Universal Salvation |
|---|---|---|---|
| Philippians Chapter 2 | *God all in all*:<br><br>Every knee in heaven and on earth and under the earth will bow to God (verses 10–11). | *Purification*:<br><br>Paul clarifies that all souls will be singing praises to God at this time in the book of Romans (Romans, chapter 14, verse 11). | Universal Salvation |

Jonathon shared his findings with his wife. "Honey, I just finished the assignment the professor gave us. This is so amazing. Now it's clear to me that Paul prophesied about the divine perfection of the universe in five of the books he wrote. The professor was right, the elephant was always right in front of my eyes, but I couldn't see it behind Jerome's smoke and mirrors. I've mentally jumped over these passages each and every time I read the Bible!"

Samantha was both enthusiastic and surprised. "But did you also check for the 'method used to get there'?" she asked.

"Yes, and that's the best part. In Paul's final-state descriptions, every single human soul is shown mercy, is put under the authority of Christ, is reconciled to God through Christ, and ends up singing praises to God. That all sounds like universal salvation—the salvation of every soul!"

With those words, Samantha suddenly flashed back to the horrible day Jamie was taken from her. She recalled the wave of peace that overtook her body when she prayed, "God, *I trust you with the salvation of my son.*" Then she began to wonder: "Is it possible that God has arranged all the events necessary for Jonathon and me to learn about universal salvation? Is this God's way of answering my prayer? Is God trying to show me that he has already worked out a plan to reconcile everyone, including Jamie?"

Samantha's depression began to lift as she considered the possibilities.

¤ ¤ ¤

The first thing Samantha did when she got home on Friday was to call Grace. But Grace didn't answer, and she didn't return the call. Samantha knew it must have been related to Jonathon's phone call with Mark.

Samantha cried herself to sleep, wondering whether she had lost her lifelong friend.

¤ ¤ ¤

The next morning Mark and Grace had an intense argument.

"Mark, I really need to talk to Samantha," Grace insisted. "If Jonathon has gone off the deep end like you say, then Samantha needs my support more than ever."

After further heated discussion, Mark reluctantly suggested, "Perhaps you could arrange to talk to Samantha at the same time the pastor meets with Jonathon today."

"Great," Grace gleefully replied. "I'm going to call her right now."

Mark responded sternly, "Wait a minute. I want to remind you that if Jonathon doesn't change his mind, then for our family's sake, we will have to distance ourselves from Jonathon and Samantha *both.*"

"I'm going to call Samantha," Grace sadly replied. "Let's pray that today becomes a turning point for the Webbers."

¤ ¤ ¤

On Saturday afternoon, Jonathon went to meet the pastor in his study as they had agreed. When he reached the entrance to the pastor's office, the door was open, and he noticed an older gentleman inside, talking with the pastor.

Pastor Rick looked up. "Hi, Jonathon, please come in."

Jonathon entered with some hesitation.

The pastor continued. "I'm sorry to spring a surprise on you. Jonathon, I'd like you to meet Harold. Harold has dedicated his life to deprogramming people who have been brainwashed by cults, including the cult of universal salvation. I was given his name from a colleague of mine at seminary."

Jonathon took a step back.

"Hi, Jonathon," Harold said, walking toward him. "I've heard that you are already convinced that universal salvation was the official doctrine of the early church and that it is what the Greek manuscript of the Bible teaches. But what if I told you that I have spoken to dozens of people who believed exactly what you do, and that they all changed their minds when I showed them 'the death knell of universal salvation'? Do you mind if we talk a little, Jonathon?"

# Chapter Twenty-One

Harold began his deprogramming maneuvers. "Jonathon, let me get straight to the point. Pastor Rick tells me you are a very rational man. In fact, he said that you are one of the most rational people he knows."

Jonathon nodded, all the while wondering where the buildup was leading to.

"So I'm sure that when I show you a rational reason why universal salvation contradicts the Bible's book of Matthew, you will accept the truth."

"I'm certainly willing to listen," Jonathon said. "Why are you emphasizing rationality?"

"Because whenever the Bible places two things in parallel, the only *rational* way to interpret them is according to their parallelism."

"I'm not following you. What is 'parallelism'?" Jonathon replied.

Harold grinned. "Let me explain by giving you an example right out of the Bible itself—from the book of Matthew."

Harold handed Jonathon a Bible, and pointed to a sentence in the twenty-fifth chapter of the book of Matthew:

*"These will go away into **eternal punishment**, but the righteous into **eternal life**."*

Harold's grin widened from ear to ear. "In this sentence, the Bible uses the same Greek word—aionios—to describe both the punishment and the reward. In other words, the Bible is placing the duration of the reward (aionios life) in parallel with the duration of the punishment (aionios punishment). So therefore, we have to keep them parallel when we translate them both into English. In other words, if you insist that the penalty is only *temporary* punishment, then you must also insist that the reward is only *temporary* life. But, if you agree that the reward is *eternal* life, then rationality forces you to agree that the penalty is *eternal* punishment as well. There simply are no other alternatives."

Jonathon read the sentence over and over again before finally conceding. "Okay, rationality forces me to agree with you, Harold. The Bible clearly puts the reward in parallel with the penalty. And any rational translation has to keep them parallel."

Harold leaned back confidently in his chair.

Jonathon closed his eyes and uttered a prayer. "God, I'm confused right now. How can I reconcile this parallel found in Matthew with the many passages I read on the plane written by Paul?" All of a sudden, Jonathon opened his eyes and enthusiastically declared, "Oh my God! Parallels aren't the death knell of universal salvation at all! In fact, they are the *key* to universal salvation. The early Christians believed that every soul will be reconciled to God *because of the Bible's parallels*—the parallels found in Paul's writings."

"What are you talking about?" Harold asked suspiciously.

Jonathon explained, "In Romans chapter eleven, Paul wrote, "For God has shut up all in disobedience so that He may show mercy to all." In other words, Paul put the number of people who are made disobedient 'in parallel with' the number who are shown mercy. The only rational way to interpret his statement is to keep them parallel. And since *all* have been made disobedient therefore *all* will be shown mercy."

"Yes, but—" Harold tried to interject.

But Jonathon plowed forward. "And in the fifteenth chapter of First Corinthians Paul wrote, "For as in Adam all die, so also in Christ all will be made alive." In other words, Paul put the number of people who are made dead in Adam 'in parallel with' the number who are made alive in Christ. And Paul even repeated this same parallel in the fifth chapter of Romans. So Paul wrote about the same parallel *twice* to make sure Christians understand that since *everyone* is made dead in Adam, *everyone* will be made alive in Christ! I agree, Harold, when the Bible puts things in parallel, rationality demands that we keep the translation in parallel as well!"

"Okay, but—" Harold said, trying once again to get a word in edgewise.

But Jonathon just kept going. "Paul also wrote about yet another parallel in the fifteenth chapter of First Corinthians. Paul wrote, "When all things are subjected to the Son, then the Son Himself also will be subjected to [God], the One who subjected all things to Him." Here Paul puts God's enemies' final relationship with Christ 'in parallel with' Christ's final relationship with God the Father. So the only rational interpretation is to conclude that God's enemies ultimately end up as God's friends!"

The pastor stepped in. "Jonathon, you still haven't addressed the parallel in Matthew. Are you avoiding it because you have no answer?"

Jonathon responded, "Pastor, forgive what I'm going to say, but you're the one who's doing the avoiding. You've just ignored four parallels in an attempt to cling to one."

The pastor leaned back in his chair. "So you don't have an answer for the Matthew passage?"

Jonathon sighed, then looked the pastor in the eyes. "Pastor, do you remember when you asked me to have a Greek scholar translate the phrase 'aionios kolasis'?"

"Yes."

"And do you remember what the scholar said was the most common Hellenistic meaning of the word *aionios*?"

"Yes, I remember," the pastor responded. "He claimed that the primary meaning was 'lasting for an age.'"

"Well, Pastor, I went to the site the professor gave, to double-check his answer. And sure enough, he was telling the truth," Jonathon declared.

"I studied basic Greek in seminary," the pastor reminded Jonathon. "And I learned that there is no higher authority on the ancient Greek language than the lexicon written by Liddell and Scott, which I have here on my bookshelf."

With that, the pastor leapt out of his chair and grabbed a copy of *A Greek English Lexicon*—the foremost standard reference for the ancient Greek language. He opened it, found the entry for *aionios*, and started reading it to himself. Within seconds, his face turned pale. He tossed the book onto his desk.

Harold reached over and read the first few words out loud, "Lasting for an age."

There was total silence. A couple of minutes later, Harold defiantly said to Jonathon, "But my original question still remains. How can you interpret the Matthew passage using this meaning without denying the reward of eternal life?"

Jonathon calmly replied, "By interpreting the passage the same way the early Christians did. The early Christians believed that every soul is immortal—or, in other words, already has eternal life. But they also believed that there is going to be a temporary separation of these eternal souls immediately after the resurrection. Some eternal souls rise to enjoy a special reward during an age, or eon, when Jesus reigns supreme. The other eternal souls receive fiery punishment during this same eon. But by the time the eon is over, all souls will have been reconciled to God, with the eon of punishment and special reward having come to an end."

The pastor choked as he said, "So the early Christians believed in a separation that 'lasted for an age,' during which the righteous enjoy the reward of *eonion* life and the unrighteous endure the penalty of *eonion* punishment? And that's how they maintained the parallel found in Matthew while also affirming eternal life?"

Jonathon nodded his head as he said, "Precisely."

Harold raised his hand. "But, Jonathon, the interpretation I'm convinced of—eternal life and eternal punishment—also keeps the phrases parallel. But I must admit yours does too. I guess we're at a stalemate."

Staring directly into Harold's eyes, Jonathon boldly declared, "No, Harold, we are not at a stalemate at all. Your interpretation contradicts the four biblical parallels I mentioned earlier, while mine does not. To accept your translation would require me to deny the other four parallels found in scripture. As a 'rational' man, I must uphold *every* parallel. I cannot choose to interpret one parallel to the detriment of four others, especially when there is a viable translation that maintains them all."

The pastor looked at Harold, and Jonathon could tell he was waiting for a comeback. But none came.

After a long period of silence, Jonathon turned to the pastor and said, "This guy is unbelievable. He walked in here ready to accuse me of being 'irrational' and 'brainwashed' if I rejected just one parallel that he showed me in the Bible.   Yet when I use his same standard, four times over, *he* still doesn't budge. Now that's a classic case of brainwashing."

Jonathon folded his arms across his chest and waited patiently for Harold's response.

# Chapter Twenty-Two

Grace arrived at the Webbers' home shortly after Jonathon left to meet with Pastor Rick.

"I'm so concerned about you, Samantha," Grace said after her friend greeted her at the door.

"Please don't worry about me," Samantha responded. "I know a couple of weeks ago I told you I was suffering from severe depression, but I'm much better now."

Grace was glad not only to hear Samantha's words but to see how much she really meant it. "I don't know how you do it," she said. "On top of dealing with the loss of your son, you now have to deal with your husband doubting the Bible. Yet you really look much better."

Samantha struggled for words. She hadn't told Grace about all she had learned. "Grace ... I ... Well, Jonathon and I ..."

Grace placed her hand gently on Samantha's shoulder. "What is it? You can tell me anything. What's bothering you?"

The words flew out of Samantha's mouth. "I no longer believe that the punishment in hell lasts forever. I now believe that the souls of the unrighteous become repentant in the fires, and then they rise out to join in the Kingdom of God."

"Oh, Samantha!" Grace exclaimed. "If that's what you have to believe to deal with your son's death, I'm not going to argue with you, as long as this belief doesn't affect your own faith in Jesus."

Samantha responded, "Actually, my new understanding has only strengthened my faith in Jesus. But it has severely weakened my confidence in our church."

Grace couldn't believe her ears. "Samantha, you don't have to stop believing in our church just because of this one issue," she exclaimed.

"But, Grace," Samantha gently responded, "this one issue changes the way I see everything."

"Like what?" Grace asked.

"Well, for one thing, it dramatically changes the way I view the nature of God."

"What does your belief in universal salvation have to do with God's nature?" Grace asked.

"In the book of Matthew, Jesus said that everyone, even evil people, treat their loved ones very well," Samantha explained. "He then taught that *a person's true nature is only revealed by the way they treat their enemies.*"

Grace was incredulous. "But hold on, Samantha, even though I believe in hell, I also believe that God is a God of love," she said. "I keep the two separate."

Samantha sighed. "Grace, as much as you may think you can separate the two, Jesus's teaching in Matthew says you really cannot. And as a matter of fact, Jesus also taught anyone who believes that the unrighteous deserve to be destroyed with fire does not even know the Holy Spirit."

Grace became irritated by the implications of Samantha's statement. "I don't know where you get some of your crazy ideas! *Of course* I know the Holy Spirit. So there's no way the Bible could say that!"

Without another word, Samantha went to the den and returned with the Bible. When she returned, she read from the ninth chapter of the book of Luke:

> When His disciples James and John saw this, they said, "Lord, do You want us to command fire to come down from heaven and consume them?"
>
> But [Jesus] turned and rebuked them, and said, "**You do not know what kind of spirit you are of**; for the Son of Man did not come to destroy men's lives, but to save them."

With those words, Grace only became more agitated. "But, Samantha, it's not God who forces people into hell. People choose to go there."

Samantha's patience was beginning to wear thin. "Really? Do people jump into the fire, or are they cast into it? And, Grace, who casts the souls into the fire?"

"God," Grace answered faintly.

"And doesn't the Bible also say the unrighteous will eventually bow their knees, swear allegiance to God, and profess Jesus is the Christ?"

Grace perked back up. "Well, yes, after they are forced to."

"Of course after they are forced to," Samantha responded. "But you say that after they've finally sworn their allegiance to God he's going to cast them into an eternal fire anyway. Yet he's still a God of love."

"Well, that part has always confused me," Grace admitted.

"Well of course it confuses you, because in your heart you know these two concepts are logically impossible!"

"I wouldn't go that far," Grace answered defensively.

"Let me put it another way," Samantha said. "Just for a moment, pretend that God had indeed planned for the salvation of every soul in the universe even before the world began. As part of his plan, he becomes flesh and tells the world there are two paths to becoming reconciled to him. If people submit to his Spirit, they will be saved from eonion punishment in Gehenna and go straight into the Kingdom of God. Otherwise, people must endure severe wrath and chastisement in the fires of Gehenna."

Grace nodded, indicating that she was fully engaged.

Samantha continued, "After teaching this, God takes on the sins of the whole world and sacrifices himself, paying the full price for every soul. Then, two thousand years later, there's a group of people telling others that they must submit to God, or else he's going to torture them for all eternity. Of course God would say, 'Hey, if you believe that, you really don't know what I'm all about. You've got me all wrong.'"

"Oh, Samantha, you've swallowed this stuff far more than I could have imagined. I'm going to miss you," Grace said, before turning around and walking out the door.

Samantha was trembling with hurt and disappointment. She knew she would probably never see Grace again.

¤ ¤ ¤

Pastor Rick turned to Harold. "I appreciate you taking the time to speak with us today. Do you mind if I talk to Jonathon alone now?"

"I hope I was of some help," Harold replied. "Good-bye," he said as he hurried out the door.

After Harold left, Pastor Rick told Jonathon, "I don't want to debate this universal salvation thing anymore. Besides, there is a more important topic for us to discuss, and that is your faith in the Bible itself."

"But, Pastor," Jonathon answered, "we can't separate our discussion of universal salvation from the construction of the modern Bible. The modern version of the Bible was purposefully manufactured to suppress the doctrine of universal salvation. When Jerome wrote the Latin Vulgate, he added two fraudulent books to the Bible—Second Peter and Jude. He swapped the original version of the Old Testament with another one. He changed the Greek word 'aionios' to 'eternal' in the original books of the New Testament. And he even removed references to universal salvation from the writings of the early fathers. He did all of this to make Christians interpret the words of the original Bible in a whole new way."

The pastor balked. "Jonathon, you're talking about a conspiracy. Give me a break!"

"I'm serious, Pastor," Jonathon replied. "And your whole view of the afterlife is based on Jerome's fabricated Bible, not on the actual teachings of Jesus."

The pastor raised his voice. "Jonathon, you're really going way out there. Evangelical Christianity is founded on the truth that every book in the Bible is the inspired word of God."

"But which Bible, Pastor? Why do you place all your trust in the *modern* Bible instead of the *apostolic* Bible? Can you show me one place where Jesus said that Second Peter is an authentic book of the

Bible?" Jonathon asked.

"Of course I can't," the pastor replied. "But the Holy Spirit guided the early church to know which books were inspired and which ones were not. I trust the books chosen by the early church."

"No, Pastor," Jonathon said with exasperation, "I am the one who trusts the books selected by the early church, while you place your faith instead on the collection of books chosen by Jerome *against the wisdom of all the apostolic fathers.* And Christianity continues to suffer grave consequences for promoting Jerome's Bible as 'the Bible'. Because of Jerome's Bible, Christians now see God as a being who inflicts eternal suffering on everyone who doesn't follow him. This is a different God than the one Jesus taught about."

The pastor frowned. "Jonathon, I refuse to question the Bible that is used by hundreds of millions of Christians. And I'm sorry, but I have no choice but to relieve you of all your responsibilities at the church, including removing your name from the membership roll. I hope Samantha understands, and I hope someday she can get through to you."

"I understand, Pastor," Jonathon said as he rose from the chair. He shook the pastor's hand before leaving the church, never to return.

¤ ¤ ¤

On Sunday morning, Peter awoke to the sound of the television, which he had left on the night before. His bleary eyes saw the image of a man throwing himself off the Bay Bridge as he heard the reporter say, "This footage was captured by a tourist early this morning. Today's suicide brings this year's total to thirty-six known jumps."

Peter thought, "That'll do it. I'll be number thirty-seven." So he got out of bed and desperately began writing his suicide note: "To whoever finds this. I have no friends or family. Bury my body wherever you want."

Peter took the note and put it inside a small plastic bag. Then using duct tape he found in the garage, he securely wrapped the plastic-encased note around his right leg.

# Chapter Twenty-Three

The phone rang early Sunday morning at the Webber household. Samantha answered it. It was Dr. Richmond.

"Hello, Samantha. I was calling to see how the two of you are doing."

"We're doing well. We're getting ready for church now. How are you?"

"Church?" Dr. Richmond remarked. "Are you telling me that you and Jonathon have remained Christians after all you've learned?"

Samantha laughed. "Of course. In fact, thanks to you, I feel like we're just beginning to discover the genuine Christian faith that existed before the Jerome conspiracy. We've located a church that has reconstructed the original apostolic Bible—they use an Old Testament based on the Greek Septuagint, the New Testament books are restricted to the apostolic canon, and the entire Bible is translated using the common vernacular meaning of each Hellenistic Greek word instead of the 'special meanings' theologians have assigned to them. Jonathon and I are so excited to go and worship there."

"I can hear the excitement in your voice. And I'm glad to hear it," Dr. Richmond affirmed.

Samantha gently responded, "Don, we'll be praying for your soul. We hope you find the truth that is in Christ one day."

"I appreciate your concern for my well-being," Dr. Richmond sincerely replied.

"And we appreciate your concern for us. I have to go now; I don't want to be late for church. Jonathon and I will call you later this week. We'd love to take you to dinner when we go to San Francisco to claim Jamie's belongings."

"That would be nice."

With that, Samantha hung up the phone and continued getting ready for church.

¤ ¤ ¤

Samantha and Jonathon entered the Church of the Apostolic Fathers, the church Samantha had discovered a week ago while conducting her Internet search. When they entered the foyer, the pastor came over and greeted them.

"Hello, Samantha," the pastor said warmly as he shook her hand. "I'm so glad you chose to come by."

Samantha introduced the pastor to her husband. Then, with a disturbed look, she said, "Pastor, I have a question about something that has been troubling me. Can you tell me when we might be able to talk next?"

"Sure. Instead of attending Sunday school, why don't we all go into my office?"

The three went into the pastor's study.

Samantha began. "Pastor, our son Jaime was gay and we recently lost him to a car accident. I know that Paul wrote 'no homosexual shall enter the kingdom of God.' And it pains me to think how much he's going to suffer in Gehenna because of this. Just how long does the Bible say he'll be there for being gay?"

"Samantha, you must always remember the Bible was written in Greek," the pastor responded.

"I know that!" Samantha immediately replied.

"Great!" the pastor affirmed. "So who did the Bible say cannot enter the kingdom of heaven?"

"No homosexual," Samantha repeated.

"That's English, Samantha," the pastor chided. "Who did the Bible say cannot enter the kingdom of heaven?"

Samantha sat thinking for a moment before a puzzled look crossed her face. "I don't know?"

"The Bible says no *arsenokoitai* shall enter the kingdom of God," said the pastor. "And every Koine Greek source on record (including

Christian works such as the *Sybilline Oracles* and *The Acts of John*) applied this word to child molesters—not homosexuals. There isn't a single Koine source that used this word in reference to same sex adult coupling—not one."

"It'll take time for us to look at the biblical texts to see if what you are saying is true," Jonathon interjected. "But I sure have seen a mountain of documentation that has been swept under the rug in order to rewrite 'eternal punishment' into the Bible. So it would no longer surprise me to discover other teachings have been added as well."

The pastor smiled. "And that's exactly the attitude we encourage in this church. I never want you to take my word for anything. Always, always, always go to the original Koine Greek and find out for yourself." The pastor placed his hand on Samantha's shoulder. "And I'm confident that once you do check things out for yourself, you'll be pleasantly surprised what the scriptures actually say about your gay son."[51]

The Webbers thanked the pastor for his time. Then they left for the sanctuary.

¤ ¤ ¤

Meanwhile, Peter was already halfway to the bridge. He stopped for a moment, raised his right pant leg, and made sure that the suicide note was still securely fastened. He then continued walking, more desperate than ever to end his miserable life.

¤ ¤ ¤

Samantha and Jonathon noticed that the morning service was very similar in format to the services held at their previous church: they sang, they prayed, they listened to the choir. And after the choir finished, the pastor rose to start his sermon.

---

51 See *The Jesus Secret* by Michael Wood, Chapter 12.

¤ ¤ ¤

Peter had been walking for almost two and a half hours. His desperation intensified when he reached the point where he could finally see the bridge in the distance. He figured that in just a little more than half an hour, it would all be over.

¤ ¤ ¤

The pastor began preaching. "The Holy Spirit had guided me today to preach on anger and the need to settle matters quickly with everyone we are angry with. I am going to be preaching from the book of Matthew, chapter five, verses twenty-one to twenty-six, which reads:

> You have heard that the ancients were told, "YOU SHALL NOT COMMIT MURDER" and "Whoever commits murder shall be liable to the court."
>
> **But I say to you that everyone who is angry with his brother shall be guilty** before the court; and whoever says to his brother, "You good-for-nothing," shall be guilty before the supreme court; and whoever says, "You fool," shall be **guilty enough to go into the fires of Gehenna**.
>
> Therefore if you are presenting your offering at the altar, and there remember that your brother has something against you, leave your offering there before the altar and go; **first be reconciled to your brother**, and then come and present your offering.
>
> **Make friends quickly with your opponent** at law while you are with him on the way, so that your opponent may not hand you over to the judge, and the judge to the officer, and you be thrown into prison.
>
> **Truly I say to you, you will not come out of there until you have paid up the last cent.**

"According to this passage, any anger we have inside of us when we die will prevent us from entering the kingdom of God. If our soul is tainted by anger, then our soul will need to be purified in the fires of Gehenna, and we will not get out until we have paid the very last cent—that is, until we are perfected in love. Perfection in love is always the requirement for entrance into the kingdom of God." The pastor paused for dramatic effect.

¤ ¤ ¤

When Peter reached the foot of the bridge, his determination wavered for a moment. "Do I really want to do this?" he wondered. Then he thought about his parents' disownment, Jamie's death, and how alone he had been for the last three weeks. "No one cares whether I live or not," he concluded. "So why should I?" Peter stepped onto the eight-mile-long bridge and started walking, looking for a place where he could climb the fence and throw himself into the turbulent waters below.

# Chapter Twenty-Four

After the pastor finished his sermon, he ended the morning service with a prayer. "God, may your Holy Spirit reveal to each and every one of us the names of the people we are angry with. Teach us to surrender our anger to your Spirit of perfect love. Give us wisdom to know what we must do to set things right with our brothers while we still have time. In Jesus's name, amen."

¤ ¤ ¤

Peter found his jumping point. Bending down, he checked one last time to make sure the note was secure. As he stood up, he looked around to see whether anyone was walking nearby.

"No one is close, now's the time to do it," he told himself, and he began climbing the barrier between him and the fatal fall to the water below.

As Peter reached the top, desperate tears streamed down his face. He heard a scream in the distance. "Oh, my God!" a woman yelled. "Someone's going to jump!"

Peter realized that he had to let go right away, before anyone reached him. He looked to the sky and said, "Good-bye." Then, the moment he began to release his grip, his cell phone started ringing.

The ringing phone gave him pause. "What the …? I haven't received a single call in three weeks," he thought.

Peter wobbled back and forth on top of the fence, hanging in the balance between life and death. He reached into his jacket with one hand, while trying to keep his balance with the other. When he brought the phone close to his face, he was surprised to see who was calling him. It was Jonathon Webber. As he continued wobbling back and forth, he pressed the green button on his phone.

"Yes?" he answered.

"Hello, Peter," Jonathon began. "This morning while I was in church, the Holy Spirit showed me that I have been holding a lot of anger against you. And he put it in my heart to make things right with you as soon as possible. In fact, I'm sitting in the church parking lot, and I felt I couldn't leave without resolving this with you."

"Okay," was all Peter could say as he looked down at the dark, distant waters below, still determined to let go.

Jonathon continued. "Peter, I know you are estranged from your own parents. And you are the one who took care of our son while he was alive. Is there any chance you would want to come visit us for a week or so? Samantha and I both would like to get to know you, and we'd also like the opportunity to learn more about our son ... We hardly talked to him after he moved in with you."

"Yes, I would like that," Peter replied through his confusion.

Jonathon began stuttering as he said from the bottom of his heart, "Peter, can you forgive me? I was so angry and my anger blinded me from seeing you as a child who Christ died for. I truly am so sorry."

With those words, Peter began leaning in the direction of the sidewalk, to make sure he didn't accidentally fall to the other side. "Yes, Mr. Webber, I forgive you." He then allowed the phone to drop to the sidewalk, so he could use both hands to maintain his balance and climb back down. When he reached the bottom, he called Jonathon back to set a date to go visit the Webbers.

During his long walk home, Peter determined to get his life in order. The first thing he did when he got to the house was to start straightening it up. And then he began opening the mail that had been piling up for the last three weeks.

As he was reading his mail, he came across a letter addressed to him from Jamie's attorney. The letter informed him that he was Jamie's sole heir and that he also was listed as the sole beneficiary on Jamie's life insurance policy. He made an instant decision to use some of the money to check himself into rehab so he could be clean by the time he went to visit the Webbers.

¤ ¤ ¤

Samantha joined Jonathon in bed to read the book of Colossians, a book of the Bible written by Paul. She particularly enjoyed the passage in chapter one, where Paul prophesied that everyone God created will be reconciled back to him. After finishing the book, she reached over and turned out the light.

Samantha fell asleep with Paul's promise of universal reconciliation on her mind. And it wasn't long before she started dreaming. While her dreams typically faded in and out, this night she had an unusually lucid dream. It felt so real.

Samantha dreamed that she and Jonathon were enjoying life in paradise, in the Kingdom of God. And every evening, there was an incredible banquet, with Jesus sitting at the head of an immense table. The table stretches for miles, allowing it to accommodate every inhabitant of the Kingdom.

Samantha noticed that every evening the guests were assigned one seat closer to the head of the table, so that everyone eventually got to sit next to Jesus. The guests' names were engraved on golden placards placed around the table, indicating who sat where.

One evening, however, when she and Jonathon entered the banquet hall, the angels took them to seats much farther away from the head of the table than they had been the night before.

After taking her seat, Samantha turned to one of the angels and asked, "Why have we been moved so far down the table? Have we done something wrong?"

The angel laughed and cheerfully replied, "We just thought you might want to sit here at this part of the table tonight."

Just then, the nightly announcement resounded throughout the banquet hall: "New arrivals!" All the inhabitants cheered every night when that announcement was made.

Samantha turned to her right and noticed the empty chair next to her. Curious, she reached for the golden placard to see the name of the person who was going to sit beside her. As she gazed at the name, her hands started trembling, and tears of joy danced on her face.

"Jonathon! Jonathon!" she shouted, showing him the placard. "Look!"

Jonathon laughed and hugged her. Tears flowed from his eyes as he continued to stare at the name engraved on the golden placard— for the name on the placard was the name of his son ... Jamie Webber.

The emotional impact of the dream woke Samantha up. She was sobbing tears of joy as the weight of Jamie's death lifted from her shoulders. She gazed upward, wiped the tears from her eyes, and then whispered warmly into the night, "I'll see you in heaven, my love."

THE END

# Appendix A
# Koine Greek Word Studies

### Gehenna

When Jesus walked the earth, the Jews threw their garbage into the valley just outside the city of Jerusalem. The name of this valley was Gehenna. The garbage in Gehenna burned day and night—its fire never came to an end.

In addition to continual fire, the Gehenna garbage dump was constantly teaming with maggots which feasted on the constant supply of discarded animal parts. In the valley called Gehenna, just outside the city of Jerusalem, the fire never came to an end and the worm population never died.

Why this geography lesson? Because the word translated as 'hell' in the modern Bible is the Greek word 'Gehenna'—the name of the garbage dump just outside of Jerusalem. According to modern Bibles, Jesus supposedly said:

> **Hell**, where their worm does not die, and the fire is not quenched.—Mark 9:47c-48 NASB

But what Jesus actually said was:

> **Gehenna**, where their worm does not die and their fire is not quenched.—Mark 9:47c-48 Literal Greek

Why is the wording so important? It's important because there is only one place in the entire Jewish scriptures where Gehenna is mentioned. So we don't have to sift through a lot of information to figure out what the Jews believed about it. For it is mentioned only once.

Gehenna is described in the prophet Isaiah's prophecy regarding the New Heaven and New Earth. In this prophecy he describes the New Jerusalem, and he gives a prophecy about the valley outside it. He describes the valley of Gehenna. Regarding Gehenna, Isaiah prophesied:

> And **it shall be from new moon to new moon** ... their worm will not die and their fire will not be quenched.—Isaiah 66:22-23 NASB

Most Christians are not aware that Jesus quoted from the prophet Isaiah's prophecy when he spoke of "Gehenna, where their worm will not die and their fire will not be quenched." And they are even less aware that Isaiah's prophecy says their worm will not die *from new moon to new moon* and their fire will not be quenched *from new moon to new moon*. Most Christians are unaware there was a specified time limit.

So what exactly is the amount of time expressed by the phrase "new moon to new moon"? The answer is quite simple. The early Jews measure time based on lunar cycles. The period of one lunar year was one new moon to its same new moon. The prophet Isaiah symbolized the time limit of Gehenna as one lunar year. In modern English, Isaiah's prophecy reads:

> And **it shall be for twelve months** ... their worm will not die and their fire will not be quenched.

So that's how the passage really reads? Absolutely. And this is why the early Jewish Rabbinic literature said:

> The punishment of the wicked in **Gehenna is twelve months.**—Shabbat 33b

And another early Jewish Rabbinic writing said:

> The judgment of the unrighteous in **Gehenna shall endure twelve months**, for it is written, "It will be from one moon until its moon."—Eduyoth 2:10

The Rabbinic author above understood the reference to the lunar year, for the above author wrote at a time when the Jews still measured time based on lunar cycles. Unfortunately, modern translators are unfamiliar with the early Jewish lunar cycles and therefore do not convert the Jewish idiom into a modern English equivalent.

Conversion of cultural idioms is an absolute essential of proper translation. But proper translation certainly creates a dilemma. For the Christian believer must assume that Jesus would never contradict Isaiah. The Christian believer must assume that Jesus and Isaiah were in total agreement. Therefore the Christian believer must conclude that Jesus was speaking about the symbolic twelve months where their worm shall not die and their fire will not be quenched. How long exactly? I guess we'll never know. But certainly a symbolic twelve months doesn't even begin to support the notion of a punishment that lasts for eternity.

## Hades

Did you know the King James Bible says Jesus went straight to hell after being crucified?

> He seeing this before spake of the resurrection of Christ, that his soul was not left in **hell**, neither his flesh did see corruption. (Acts 2:31 KJV)

So does the original Bible—the Koine Greek Bible—say Jesus went straight to hell after his crucifixion? No, it does not. The Koine Greek Bible says Jesus went to *Hades*—the holding place of souls.

According to the Koine Greek Bible every soul (including Jesus's) goes to Hades after death. The Koine Bible says that souls normally stay there until judgment day (with some exceptions such as Jesus's resurrection). The Koine Bible also says that Hades will one day be emptied and it itself will be destroyed in a future lake of fire:

> Then death and **Hades** were thrown into the lake of fire (Revelation 20:14 NASB)

It is always important to remember that the Koine Bible says that Hades will be destroyed (i.e. Hades' existence is temporary). Why is this important? Many Christians wrongly believe that the story of the Rich Man and Lazarus teaches about a God who inflicts eternal punishment. They get this idea from the mistranslated King James Bible.

> The rich man also died, and was buried; And in **hell** he lift up his eyes, being in torments, and seeth Abraham afar off, and Lazarus in his bosom. (Luke 16:22-23 KJV)

I'm sure you can guess which word was mistranslated here. Fortunately, the NASB Bible has restored the mistranslation.

> The rich man also died and was buried. In **Hades** he lifted up his eyes, being in torment, and saw Abraham far away and Lazarus in his bosom. (Luke 16:22-23 NASB)

The story of the Rich Man and Lazarus mentions a chasm that prevents souls from traveling from one place to another.

> And besides all this, between us and you there is a great chasm fixed, so that those who wish to come over from here to you will not be able, and that none may cross over from there to us.' (Luke 16:26 NASB)

For five hundred years, people were told that this uncrossable chasm was a part of hell itself (thanks to the King James' mistranslation). For centuries people were warned that this fixed chasm 'in hell' proves that the fires of hell burn forever and no one can escape. They did not know the Koine Bible says that Hades (and the chasm fixed within it) are temporary. Can you imagine how many tens of thousands of scary sermons were based on this mistranslation over a five hundred year period?

Most Christians are unaware that the mainstream view of the original Christians was purgatory—not hell. The majority of original Christians couldn't conceive of a God who inflicted a punishment that lasted for all eternity. They viewed such a God as the opposite of the one taught by Jesus of Nazareth.

Why did they believe this? The Koine Greek Bible does not have a single reference to eternal punishment. Not one.

## Hupotasso

The Koine word *hupotasso* meant 'to be submitted to the will of another'. The meaning of this word is beautifully illustrated by the following passage.

> And Jesus went down with his parents and came to Nazareth, and he continued **in subjection** to them; and his mother treasured all these things in her heart.—Luke 2:51

In this passage, Jesus was "in subjection" [*hupotasso*] to his parents. In other words, Jesus was "submitted to their will". Let's examine another passage.

> Therefore it is necessary to be **in subjection**, not only because of wrath, but also for conscience' sake.—Romans 13:5

In this passage, Christians are told to "be in subjection" (be submitted to the will) [*hupotasso*] of the government. Now consider one more example.

> that you also be **in subjection** to such men and to everyone who helps in the work and labors.—1 Corinthians 16:16

In this passage, Christians are told to "be in subjection" (be submitted to the will) [*hupotasso*] of Christian leaders.

By this point you now have a good grasp on the meaning of *hupotasso*: to be submitted to the will of another. So why is this important? The Koine Bible uses this word to describe the relationship that Christ's enemies will eventually have with Christ himself.

> For Christ must reign until he has put all his enemies under his feet... [Until] he has put all things **in subjection** under his feet ... When all things are **in subjection** to the Son, then the Son will **subject** himself to the one who **subjected** all things to him, so that God may be all in all.—1 Corinthians 15:25, 27a, 28

The above passage could be called the *hupotasso* passage. For this Koine word flows throughout it. And notice how it describes a very different final state of the universe than is taught in Catholic and Protestant churches alike. The apostle Paul wrote that Christ will eventually force all his enemies to be submitted to his will and then he will submit himself to the will of God the father (thereby making God all in all).

How interesting that the apostle Paul wrote that the enemies of Christ will have the same relationship to Christ that Christ has with the Father. How interesting that the apostle Paul envisions an end game in which the entire universe (including Christ's enemies) are all submitted to the will of God. Where is 'eternal punishment' in this schema? It simply doesn't exist.

The teaching of 'eternal punishment' opposes the loving message of the Koine Greek Bible—the only Christian Bible. The Koine Greek Bible consistently portrays God as love; a being who loves so much that he will not rest until even his enemies eventually become part of the kingdom.

## Malista

When a discussion moves from generic to a specific subset, the Koine word *malista* meant 'especially'. Let's consider a few English examples to get a good grasp on what is expressed in such generic to specific subset transitions.

> All the dresses you tried on are beautiful, especially the red one.

In the example above, the speaker transitioned from the generic (all the dresses) to a specific subset (the red one). In this instance, which of the dresses does the speaker say are beautiful? Answer: all of them. And the red one is beautiful in a special way.

Let's do another.

> I like all sports cars, especially Ferraris.

In the example above, the speaker transitioned from the generic (all sports cars) to a specific subset (Ferraris). In this instance, which sports cars does the speaker like? Answer: all of them. And he likes Ferraris in a special way.

Great. Now that you have a good grasp on the plain and simple use of 'especially' in generic to specific subset discussions, let's look at a Koine Greek example.

> the living God, who is the Savior of all men, **especially** [*malista*] of believers.—1 Timothy 4:10b

In the example above, the writer transitioned from the generic (all men) to a specific subset (believers). In this instance, who is saved by the living God? Answer: all men. And believers are saved in a special way.

Some theologians try to argue that *malista* is used as a point of emphasis in 1 Timothy 4:10, not as 'especially'. Are there valid grounds for such a statement? No. How do we know? It is the sentence structure that drives the meaning of the word. It is the transition from the generic (all men) to a specific subset (believers). In such a sentence structure *malista* has one (and only one) meaning: 'especially'.

One more time, the doctrine of 'eternal punishment' doesn't fit within Paul's schema. As pointed out in a previous blog entry, Paul taught that God will not rest until all humanity has been saved. Those who willingly accept his Law (love your neighbor as yourself) are saved in a special way and receive a special reward (life in the age to come). And Paul taught that those who currently refuse to love others now will one day (through the punishment of the age to come) be purged of their selfish ways. According to Paul, in the end, the living God is the savior of all men, especially [*malista*] of believers.

The Koine Bible consistently portrayed God as loving humanity so much that he will not rest until everyone—even his enemies—are reconciled to him.

## Dunamai

The Koine word *dunamai* meant: 'to have the capability to do something'. It's critical to note that this word expresses a capability which is completely independent of the intention of doing something. An example of this critical distinction is found in Matthew 3:9.

> "and do not suppose that you can say to yourselves, 'We have Abraham for our father'; for I say to you that from these stones God **is able to** [*dunamai*] raise up children to Abraham."—Matthew 3:9 NASB

Notice how Jesus used the Koine word *dunamai* to express God's capability completely independent of God's intention. Jesus was not threatening his audience with an actual intention of turning stones into children. He was using his belief in God's capability to do so to make a point.

Perhaps its best to translate *dunamai* consistently as 'could if he wanted to' to remind the reader that the word is expressing capability independent of intention. If we did this, Matthew 3:9 would read as follows.

> "and do not suppose that you can say to yourselves, 'We have Abraham for our father'; for I say to you that from these stones God **could if he wanted to** [*dunamai*] raise up children to Abraham."—Matthew 3:9

Now the distinction between capability and intention is much clearer.

So why is the distinction between ability and intention so important? It is important because the Koine word *dunamai* is used in one of the most misunderstood passages of the Bible.

> "Do not fear those who kill the body but are unable to kill the soul; but rather fear Him who **is able to** [*dunamai*] destroy both soul and body in hell."—Matthew 10:28 NASB

This verse is often used by modern theologians as 'proof'

that God intends to destroy souls in hell. But the verse truly says nothing about God's intention. The verse solely discusses God's ability independent of intention. All the verse says is:

> "Do not fear those who kill the body but are unable to kill the soul; but rather fear Him who **could if he wanted to** [*dunamai*] destroy both soul and body in Gehenna."—Matthew 10:28

In our previous example, we have discussed how Jesus mentioned God's capability of turning stones into children. No serious Bible scholar would use that sentence as 'proof' that God intends on turning stones into children. Yet the moment the same phraseology is applied to destroying souls in Gehenna, all the sudden it supposedly becomes 'proof' of intention to these same folks.

Ironically the earliest Christians had the opposite view of God. They believed in God who would much sooner turn stones into children than destroy souls in Gehenna. Sadly, today's theologians are so convinced of a hellish God that they even see 'proof' of their belief where none exists at all. How very powerful the indoctrinated mind is.

In the Koine Greek Bible there is not a single reference to a God who intends on inflicting eternal punishment on anyone. And there are plenty of direct statements to the contrary. There are plenty of statements that God intends on reconciling all of humanity to himself.

# The Jesus Secret

## (Preview)

# Chapter 1 -
# A Most Incredible Discovery

Most people are unaware that the translators of the first English Bibles guessed what many of the Greek words meant. They had to guess, for the first English Bibles were translated at a time when scholars didn't know the language they were translating ever even existed.

> For a long time Koine Greek confused many scholars because it was significantly different from Classical Greek. Some hypothesized that it was a combination of Greek, Hebrew, and Aramaic. Others attempted to explain it as a "Holy Ghost language," meaning that God created a special language just for the Bible. – *Greek for the Rest of Us*, by William Mounce, p. 3

For centuries scholars had never come across any document that was written in the same type of Greek as the Bible, so they assumed the Bible was written in a special language, a language made specifically and only for the Bible itself. *And the first English Bibles were translated by scholars who didn't know the language they were translating ever even existed.*

Talk about a total information vacuum. And since the scholars didn't know the biblical language, they had to guess the meanings of many important words. Of course, they took the best guesses they could. But given their complete unawareness of the prior existence of the language itself, their translation was ultimately based on many shot–in–the–dark guesses--nothing more, nothing less.

> But studies of Greek papyri found in Egypt over the last one hundred years have shown that Koine Greek was the language everyday people used in the writing of wills, letters, receipts, shopping lists, etc. – *Greek for the Rest of Us*, by William Mounce, p. 3

167

But with the dawning of the twentieth century everything was about to change. At the turn of this century archaeologists discovered so many original early Greek manuscripts that the mass of material was measured in the tons when it was shipped to London for analysis. Almost overnight, the world went from having none to literally having tons of original early Greek manuscripts. And it wasn't long before archaeologists realized one of the biggest historical surprises – these manuscripts were written using the same vocabulary, grammar and style as the Bible itself. Archaeologists discovered the Bible wasn't written in a special language after all; it was written in the native tongue of the common man. It was written in Koine Greek.

The discovery of the Koine Greek language caused a large rift to form in biblical scholarship circles. On one side were the scholars who were thrilled at the opportunity to examine the biblical texts afresh, with tons of new information to guide them in discovering teachings that might have been lost for almost two thousand years. On the other side were the traditionalists, who feared the possibility that the new material might show the church had embraced centuries of error because of poorly translated versions of the Bible.

Traditionalists have made every effort to downplay the significance of this monumental discovery, for when the wrongly guessed meanings are replaced with the actual meanings of the words, the Bible shows itself to be an entirely different document. The biblical passages come alive in surprising ways as they reveal the original Christian teachings, teachings which had been buried along with the language for almost two thousand years.

For example, the King James Bible has a rather strange reference to *evil* fruit. Fruit cannot murder. It is unable to rape. It doesn't molest children. Fruit cannot be *evil*. But if we restore the common Koine Greek meaning of the word, this passage is breathed new life, and it reveals an incredible biblical teaching that had been lost for almost two thousand years.

And consider 1 Corinthians 6:6-9. Modern English translations make it seem that Paul told the Corinthians to not bring lawsuits against each other because *the wicked* won't inherit the kingdom of

God.  Was the bringing of lawsuits really *wicked*, or did Paul possibly say something else will prevent them from inheriting the kingdom of God, something specifically related to the lawsuits themselves?  If we restore the common Koine Greek meaning of the word, this passage is given new life, and it also reveals another biblical teaching that had been lost for almost two thousand years.

Let's consider one more verse.  According to modern translations Jesus' disciple John supposedly wrote, "All *unrighteousness* is sin, and there is sin that does not lead to death."  In English, the word *unrighteousness* is itself a synonym for sin.  To the modern reader, the passage sounds like John is saying, "All sin is sin, and there is sin that doesn't lead to death"--a very confusing sentence to say the least.  However, if we restore the common Koine Greek meaning of the word the passage takes on new life.  And it reveals still another teaching that had been lost for almost two thousand years.

Word after word, sentence after sentence, passage after passage, biblical scholars analyzed the Bible in light of the actual meanings of the Koine Greek words.  During the process a large number of lost teachings were unveiled.  The Bible has shown itself to be an entirely different document than was previously believed.

Those who are avid readers of modern Bibles are likely going to be unsettled by the sudden shifts in learning that the archaeological discoveries are bringing with them.  But for those who are curious to discover the teachings of the original Christian Bible, teachings buried for almost two thousand years, welcome.

# Chapter 2 –
# Justice, Equality, and Fairness

Let me illustrate how very different the actual meanings of the Koine words are from the guesses made by the first translators. The papyri revealed that the Koine Greek word *dikaios* means: justice, equality, fairness. However the translators of the first English Bible wrongly guessed it meant: moral righteousness. Likewise, the papyri revealed another Koine Greek word, *dikaioi*, means: those who treat others justly, those who treat others equitably, those who treat others fairly. However the translators of the first English Bible wrongly guessed that it meant: those who are morally righteous.

Jesus' quintessential teaching on judgment beautifully illustrates the actual meaning of the Koine Greek word *dikaioi*.

> Then the King will say to those on his right, 'Come, you who are blessed of my father, take your inheritance in the kingdom prepared for you from the foundation of the world. **For I was hungry, and you gave me something to eat; I was thirsty, and you gave me something to drink; I was a stranger, and you invited me in; naked, and you clothed me; I was sick, and you visited me; I was in prison, and you came to Me.'**
>
> Then **the righteous** will answer Him, 'Lord, when did we see you hungry, and feed you, or thirsty, and give you something to drink? And when did we see you a stranger, and invite you in, or naked, and clothe you? When did we see you sick (or in prison) and come to you?'
> The king will answer and say to them, 'Truly I say to you, to the extent that you did it to one of these brothers of mine, even the least of them, you did it to me.' – Matthew 25:31-40 NASB

The underlined word in the passage above is the Koine Greek

word *dikaioi* in the original Christian Bible. And aren't people who feed the hungry 'those who bring justice, equality, and fairness' to the world? Aren't people who donate their extra clothes 'those who bring justice, equality, and fairness' to the world? Aren't people who shelter the homeless 'those who bring justice, equality, and fairness' to the world? Of course they are.

So we see that Jesus used the word *dikaioi* when talking about 'those who treat others justly,' 'those who treat others equitably,' and 'those who treat others fairly.' Just like the Koine papyri did. Yet, as you can see in the passage above, modern Bibles still use the discredited meaning assigned by the first translators, who didn't even know the language they were translating ever existed. Why do they do this?

Modern Bible translators have a very big dilemma. If they translate Jesus' teaching using the actual meaning of the word, then the passage would be teaching something that they themselves do not believe.

> Then the King will say to those on his right, 'Come, you who are blessed of my father, take your inheritance in the kingdom prepared for you from the foundation of the world. **For I was hungry, and you gave me something to eat; I was thirsty, and you gave me something to drink; I was a stranger, and you invited me in; naked, and you clothed me; I was sick, and you visited me; I was in prison, and you came to Me.'**
>
> Then <u>those who treated others equitably</u> will answer Him, 'Lord, when did we see you hungry, and feed you, or thirsty, and give you something to drink? And when did we see you a stranger, and invite you in, or naked, and clothe you? When did we see you sick (or in prison) and come to you?' The king will answer and say to them, 'I am telling you the truth, to the extent that you did it to one of these brothers of mine, even the least of them, you did it to me.'

When the actual meaning is restored, there is no longer any ambiguity regarding who gets life in the kingdom. (Those who treat others equitably inherit life in the kingdom.)

And we see how the actual meaning of the word seamlessly ties the passage together. Yet modern Bibles do not use the actual meaning of the word. Even though it makes the passage read seamlessly and even though it ties the entire passage together, modern Bibles don't use it. Rather they cling to the old, discredited meaning instead.

But the seamless fluidity of proper translation betrays them. No matter how much they insist on clinging to the old stab–in-the-dark meanings, all the passages in the Bible flow seamlessly the moment the actual Koine Greek meanings are applied, even the most confusing ones. Take the following passage for instance:

> If ever anyone sees his brother sinning sin not leading to death, he shall ask and God will give life for him; to the ones who do not commit sins leading to death. There is sin which leads to death (I am not saying that he should make request for this): all **unrighteousness** is sin, and there is sin which doesn't lead to death. – 1 John 5:16-17

The passage above boggles both conservative Christian camps: the Calvinists and the Armenians. Calvinists believe that once a person is saved he will always remain saved; he can never lose his salvation, no matter what he does. Armenians, on the other hand, believe people must live sinless lives if they want to keep their salvation. Calvinists do not believe in 'sins that lead to death'. Armenians do not believe in 'sins which don't lead to death'. So neither group truly understands this teaching, which contradicts them both.

And the simple reason neither group understands the teaching is because neither group reads Bibles based on the actual meanings of the Koine Greek words. Instead, both camps study Christianity from Bibles based on uninformed guesses made centuries before the Koine papyri were ever discovered. And the uninformed translators (who didn't know the language they were translating ever even existed) guessed the passage said:

> All **unrighteousness** is sin, and there is sin which doesn't lead to death.

The guessed translation of the passage can confuse anyone. After all, the English word *unrighteousness* is itself a synonym for sin. Modern Bibles make the passage appear to say all sin is sin, and yet there are other sins that don't lead to death.  Huh?

This confusing passage has resulted in centuries of theological debate.   And while theologians continued in centuries of debate, the key to understanding it rested silently for almost two millennia underneath the sands of Egypt.

# Chapter 3 –
# A Perfect Fit

For a Christian, what could be more important than understanding which sins are mortal (which sins cost your soul) and which ones aren't?

> If ever anyone sees his brother sinning sin not leading to death, he shall ask and God will give life for him; to the ones who do not commit sins leading to death. There is sin which leads to death (I am not saying that he should make request for this): all **unrighteousness** is sin, and there is sin which doesn't lead to death. – 1 John 5:16-17

How is it even possible to reconcile the modern Bible's version of John's teaching on mortal sin with Jesus' quintessential teaching on judgment? Jesus taught that those who take care of the poor and needy inherit life. Yet John appears to say that doing altruistic deeds actually isn't the deciding factor; rather, righteousness is. According to the way John's teaching reads in modern Bibles, any altruistic person who is 'unrighteous' is still committing mortal sin and therefore is destined for death. It appears that Jesus' teaching that humanity will be divided into only two groups based solely on altruism was overly simplistic ... and wrong.

The time is ripe for the church to finally face the eight hundred pound gorilla in the room. Rather than sweep the seeming inconsistencies under the rug, it's time to face them head on. Gross inconsistencies such as this are simply the natural result of translation error. The moment we restore the actual meanings of the Koine Greek words, all the textual inconsistencies vanish into thin air. And we also finally discover the original teachings of the Bible in the process, teachings that have been buried with the language for almost two thousand years.

So let's begin the biblical restoration process with the actual meanings of the words derived from *dikaios*. Let's see if Jesus' teaching on judgment and John's teaching on mortal sin really are inconsistent, or if they've simply been misunderstood for a very long time. And let's see if we might discover a lost biblical teaching as a natural part of the restoration process.

Below is a Dikaios Cheat Sheet. It is based on the way Jesus and the Koine papyri both used the word *dikaios*; therefore, you can use it to uncover the real meaning of any biblical teaching that contains any *dikaios*-based word.

## Dikaios Cheat Sheet

| | |
|---|---|
| Dikaio + s | Justice |
| | Equality |
| | Fairness |
| | |
| Dikaio + i | One who treats others justly |
| | One who treats others equitably |
| | One who treats others fairly |
| | |
| Dikaio + sune | "Justice-ness;" of justice |
| | Equitableness; of equity |
| | Fairness, of fairness |
| | |
| Dikaio + mata | Justice resulting; justice producing |
| | Equity resulting; equity producing |
| | Fairness resulting; fairness producing |
| | |
| Dikaio + krisias | A just judgment |
| | An equitable judgment |
| | A fair judgment |
| | |
| A + dikia | Unjust treatment of others |
| | Inequitable treatment of others |
| | Unfair treatment of others |
| | |
| A + dikio | One who treats others unjustly |
| | One who treats others inequitably |
| | One who treats others unfairly |

Allow me to show you how to use the Dikaios Cheat Sheet to recover the actual message John communicated to his first century Koine speaking audience. In Koine Greek, the key part of the passage reads as follows:

> **There is sin which leads to death** (I do not say that he should make request for this): all _**adikia**_ is [such] sin and there is sin which doesn't lead to death.

Using the Dikaios Cheat Sheet let's restore the actual meaning of the Koine Greek word _adikia_.

> **There is sin which leads to death** (I do not say that he should make request for this): all ***inequitable treatment of others*** is [such] sin and there is sin which doesn't lead to death.

Ah. Now the passage finally makes sense. Before we restored the Koine Greek the passage seemed to say, "All sin is sin and there is sin that doesn't lead to death"--a rather confusing sentence to say the least. But now that we've restored the actual meaning of the word, the passage makes perfect sense. The passage now reads seamlessly. And we have uncovered a biblical teaching that had been lost for two thousand years: Treating others inequitably leads to death and other sins do not.

Hmmm. Jesus taught that everyone who treats others equitably inherits life. And if this is true then only those who treat others inequitably don't inherit life. In other words, only those who treat others inequitably have committed sin that leads to death (which is exactly what John wrote). In the original Christian Bible, Jesus' teaching and John's are actually two sides of the very same coin. The moment we restored the actual meaning of the Koine Greek word, the inconsistencies vanished into thin air.

And the perfect fluidity between Jesus' teaching and John's condemns the translation found in modern Bibles. For if restoring the actual meaning of the word causes John to teach the exact same thing as Jesus, then isn't this the way the passage was meant to be translated in the first place? Of course it is. And doesn't this mean the passage has been mistranslated for centuries? Of course it does.

Modern theologians balk at translating the Bible using the actual meanings of the words. After all, the teachings which are recovered seem so foreign to them. They struggle to understand how salvation can be based solely on the way one treats his fellow man. And they struggle to understand how the only sin that can lead to death is based solely on the way one treats his fellow man. Where is man's religious obligation to God in all of this? It appears as if God has been left out of the equation.

The religious leaders of Jesus' day also thought Jesus had

ignored man's duty to God in his quintessential teaching on judgment. In fact, for these folks, when Jesus taught judgment will be based solely on neighborly altruism, he had committed heresy by leaving God out of the equation. And so the religious lawyers plotted how they could force Jesus either to retract his teaching or be stoned to death for heresy.

Jesus' disciple Matthew records a very fascinating incident where a religious lawyer publicly confronted Jesus on this. The passage is quite intriguing because the lawyer was convinced he had forced Jesus into a situation which had only two possible outcomes: either admit there is more to religion than loving our neighbors or be stoned on the spot for heresy.

> A lawyer asked Jesus a question, **testing** him, "Teacher, which is the greatest commandment in the Law?"

Do you see the trap the lawyer set? If Jesus admitted that loving God was the greatest commandment, then he would be retracting his teaching that judgment will be based entirely on loving our neighbors. But if Jesus said anything else was the greatest commandment then he would be stoned to death on the spot for heresy. What a dilemma: either admit the quintessential judgment teaching was incomplete (and therefore wrong) or be stoned for heresy. There appeared to be no good option for Jesus.

So what does the original Christian Bible say happened? Did Jesus contradict his teaching on judgment by admitting there was more to religion than loving our neighbors? Or did Jesus commit heresy by saying something else was the greatest commandment? Or is it possible that Jesus was so wise that he avoided the trap altogether by finding a surprising third option the lawyer hadn't considered?

# [End of Preview]

# The Hidden Bible

## (Preview)

# Excerpt 1

The next Sunday, Robert felt dreadfully self-conscious walking alone into the huge sanctuary of the evangelical church near campus, which was popular with the university students. Even though the ushers greeted him warmly, he felt out of place. He took a seat on the end of the aisle near the back and read the bulletin until the pastor began the service. For a few minutes, he wondered if he had made a mistake in coming, if his resolve was strong enough to do this alone — when his heart ached to have Maria by his side — and whether he could live a completely new life amongst people he did not even know. As the preparatory music stopped, indicating the service was about to begin, he felt the blush of shame, thinking of how his mother had died before seeing him saved and sitting in a true Christian church.

Right before the sermon, the pastor announced, "Every Sunday at this time, we take a moment to greet one another. Please say 'Hello' and shake the hand of everyone around you."

As soon as the organist started playing 'Because He Lives', the congregants rose to their feet to greet one another. After shaking hands with the people on his left and right, Robert turned around to find himself standing face-to-face with an exceptionally beautiful, radiant young woman. The young woman reached out her hand. "Hi! I'm Valerie."

Robert was awestruck for a moment. Quickly regaining his composure, he replied, "Hi. I'm Robert."

"Welcome, Robert. I don't recall ever seeing you here before."

"It's my first Sunday... In fact, I'm a new Christian, and just started attending church..." Robert stopped himself, feeling he was starting to ramble a bit too much.

"So, you're here alone?" Valerie asked.

"Yes. I don't have any Christian friends in town."

"Well, you've got one now." Valerie reached into her pocket and whipped out her cell phone. "Give me your number and I'll text you with mine. My dad's the pastor here. I'm staying in town at my parent's place, to save money until I leave for a missionary trip later this year. You can call me anytime with any questions you might have."

"Okay," Robert said, with a nervous smile, and then he gave her his number.

The conversation ended abruptly as the song finished, and the pastor approached the microphone ready to start the sermon.

The pastor began. "Now that we are in the end times, I find myself preaching more and more from the last book of the Bible — the book of Revelation — the book that details God's plan for the apocalyptic end of the world. And perhaps the question that I get asked the most is, 'Pastor, who is the Beast of Revelation? Who is the man represented by the devil's number, 666?' So today, I'm going to start my sermon by sharing with you what the Bible has to say about the identity of this demonic individual."

Robert was sitting on the edge of his seat.

> If anyone has insight, let him calculate the number of the Beast, for it is a man's number. His number is 666.[1]

Then the preacher explained. "The Bible says that only those who are given special insight from God can know who the Beast is. John, the author of Revelation, was telling his readers that the identity of the horrible Beast was going to remain a mystery to most of humanity until the day the Beast emerges on the scene. So, 'who is the Beast?' I don't know. And according to the Bible, I can't know. And if that's the way God wants it, then that's the way it will be."

After all that buildup, Robert felt a little deflated. Ever since becoming a Christian, he had been wondering who the Antichrist — the Beast of Revelation — was going to be. Now he realized that he was never going to know. The Bible clearly said that it was a mystery that only those with special insight would be able to know.

---

1 Revelation 13:18 NIV

¤ ¤ ¤

Over the next three weeks, Robert didn't have any contact with Maria. As badly as he wanted to be with her, he was determined to give her the space she needed to realize how wrong she had been about her church and the Bible. And he needed the time to help build his resolve to remain apart from her forever, if she refused to become saved.

Then on a Tuesday afternoon, Robert attended his Ancient Greek Language class. As a senior, much of the class was dedicated to advanced language topics, such as idioms and cultural expressions.

The teacher began. "Today, we're going to talk about the ancient Greek idiom: 'to have a mind.' The early Greeks used this expression in the same way we use the phrase 'anybody with half a brain.' In fact, the early Greeks used the opposite phrase, 'to not have a mind' when speaking about the senseless and the insane."

Robert took copious notes throughout the class, as usual. And when class ended, he rushed to his dorm room to start his daily Bible study.

Robert was delighted that the concordance showed that the Greek phrase 'to have mind' was in the Bible. And he was even more thrilled when he realized the phrase was used in the passage in Revelation that describes the identity of the dreaded Beast of Revelation. He grabbed his Greek Bible, and opened it to the passage. But when he read the sentence in Greek, applying what he had learned in class, he felt odd. Then he started feeling numb and then started shaking. He reread the sentence over and over again:

> Let **anyone who has a mind** calculate the number of the Beast. For it is a man's number. And his number is 666.[2]

In an effort to wrap his brain around what the Greek Bible said, Robert took a piece of paper and wrote out a direct translation of the sentence:

---

2   Revelation 13:18 Greek literal

Let **anybody with half a brain** calculate the number of the Beast. For it is a man's number. And his number is 666.[3]

"This doesn't make any sense," Robert said to himself. "According to the original Greek Bible, anybody with half a brain will know who the Beast of Revelation is, and only the senseless and the insane won't be able to figure it out. Not only does the original Bible say it's not a mystery — it says the answer is as obvious as the nose on the reader's face."

Robert sat for a while, thinking about the implications of what he had just read. It was then when he had his 'Eureka' moment. "If the author of Revelation expected every first century reader with half a brain to know the identity of the Beast, then he couldn't have been writing about anyone in the distant future. He must have been writing about someone they were all already familiar with — someone in the first century."

The implied logic slapped him in the face. "But the Beast of Revelation is inextricably tied to the teaching of the Rapture," he uttered. "And if the Beast of Revelation has already come and gone, that would mean there can't be any Rapture. And if that's the case, then everything I saw in that movie at Mom's church is fiction."

---

3  Revelation 13:18 Greek with idiom translated

# Excerpt 2

As Robert pondered the questions raised by the translation, he saw his phone on the desk and remembered Valerie's offer to answer any questions he might have. A quick phone call and he had a meeting that evening arranged at Sammy's, at Valerie's suggestion. Robert knew the area well, as it was only a few blocks from Maria's sorority house.

The hostess led Robert and Valerie over to a window seat. After they had both ordered, Robert explained the Greek idiom 'anyone who has a mind.' Then he showed Valerie that Revelation says that 'anybody with half a brain' will know who the Beast of Revelation is by the number 666.

Valerie was completely unfazed. "I can see why you would think the statement is mistranslated based on what you learned in class," she said with a laugh. "But when you think about it, the sentence itself shows that it truly is a mystery, not something the first century readers were expected to know."

"How can you be so sure?"

"Because, just as you said, the author of Revelation used a very cryptic, complex cipher based on the number 666. Obviously, he would never have used such an unsolvable riddle if he expected 'anybody with half a brain' to know who he was writing about."

Robert nodded. "I don't know why I didn't think of that before. It was right in front of me the whole time. I'm so glad I have you to talk to."

# Excerpt 3

The next morning, Robert was still reeling from the events at the restaurant, as he opened his books and began to do his homework. The assignment for his Greek class involved translating various passages containing the Greek idioms 'to have a mind' and 'to not have a mind.'

As Robert thought about the meanings that his teacher had given him, he became increasingly agitated. "My professor has to be wrong about the meanings of these idioms. After all, the Bible uses these expressions opposite to the way she has taught us," he said to himself.

After a couple more minutes, Robert closed his books. "I need to talk to Professor Harrison about this. She should know that she's not teaching us the correct meanings."

# Excerpt 4

"I think you might have taught us the wrong meaning of a Greek idiom," Robert nervously blurted out to his professor in her office.

Professor Harrison cracked a half smile in what seemed to Robert like bemusement. "Well, I'm always willing to learn new things, Robert. So please, tell me what my star student has discovered."

The professor's response put Robert at ease, although he wasn't sure that she was taking him seriously. "I found a first century document that uses an idiom in the exact opposite way that you said the expression was used."

"Let me tell you that I couldn't be more delighted that you're reading Greek texts above and beyond the homework I give you. So, which idiom are you talking about?"

"To have mind."

The professor leapt from her chair, walked over to the bookshelf, and grabbed two books. She flipped through the first book, a very big book. Then, pointing to an entry on a page, she said, "I assume you didn't look up the expression in a *Greek English Lexicon* by Liddell and Scott, which you know is the most authoritative dictionary of Greek. Notice the entry for the idiom 'to have mind'? Why don't you read the primary meaning aloud?"

Robert read, "To have *sense*, be *sensible*."[4]

The teacher nodded. "So, just as you learned in class, the idiom has to do with having common sense and sensibility. That's why I told you it's similar to the English slang, 'anybody with half a brain', as this slang means, 'anyone with common sense.'" The professor opened the second book entitled *In and Out of the Mind*. She pointed to a

---

4 νοῦν ἔχειν : a) to have *sense*, be *sensible*, *Greek English Lexicon*, by Liddell and Scott, p. 1180

paragraph, and once again, asked Robert to read it aloud.

> "People who act with nous [the Greek word for mind], and 'have' it, are
> sensible. People who do not are senseless, unwise, insane."[5]

The professor nodded once again. "So you see, Robert, 'to not
have mind' meant 'to be senseless, unwise, insane,' just as I taught you.
Both expressions mean exactly what you learned in class."

"But that just doesn't make any sense," Robert blurted out.
"Why then would a first century writer say anybody with half a brain
— anyone who isn't senseless or insane — would know who he was
referring to when he gave 'the man's number'?"

The teacher laughed. "But of course a first century writer
would say only a half-wit wouldn't know who he was referring to. For
in first century Greek, everyone was identified by both their name and
their number."

"I don't understand."

"In a week, we'll be discussing this topic in great detail in class.
But I'd be glad to give you a brief overview of why only an insane
individual in the first century would not know the identity of a person
by that person's number."

"Okay."

The professor walked over to her filing cabinet and pulled out
a sheet of paper with the following on it:

---

5 *In and Out of the Mind,* by Ruth Padel, 1994, p. 32

| Symbol | Character | Number |
|--------|-----------|--------|
| A | A | 1 |
| B | B | 2 |
| Γ | G | 3 |
| Δ | D | 4 |
| E | E | 5 |
| F | V, W | 6 |
| Z | Z | 7 |
| H | Ē | 8 |
| Θ | Th | 9 |
| I | I | 10 |
| K | K | 20 |
| Λ | L | 30 |
| M | M | 40 |
| N | N | 50 |
| Ξ | X | 60 |
| O | O | 70 |
| Π | P | 80 |
| Ϙ | Q | 90 |
| P | R | 100 |
| Σ | S | 200 |
| T | T | 300 |
| Υ | Y, U | 400 |
| Φ | Ph | 500 |
| X | Ch | 600 |
| Ψ | Ps | 700 |
| Ω | Ō | 800 |
| Ϡ | (Sanpi) | 900 |

The professor explained the chart. "In the first century, every Greek symbol represented both a letter and a number *at the same time.* For example, the first symbol in the chart represented both the letter 'A' and the number '1' *at the same time.* Because of this duality, the collection of symbols comprising a person's identity represented a collection of letters (the person's name) and a collection of numbers (the number of the person's name) *at the same time.*

"For example, let's consider Jesus of Nazareth, a very famous individual from the first century. Jesus was identified by the Greek symbols: **Ι Η Σ Ο Υ Σ**. And these symbols represented both Jesus' Greek name (IĒSOUS) and the number of Jesus' name (888) [10 + 8 + 200 + 70 + 400 + 200] *at the same time.* So, whenever a first century Greek saw those symbols, he thought of both Jesus' name and the number of his name each time. People's names and the number of their names were inextricably linked to one another."

"I can see from the chart that early Greek symbols were letters and numbers at the same time," Robert concurred. "But do we have any archaeological evidence that they actually used both the letters and the numbers to identify people?"

"Very good question as usual, Robert!" the professor exclaimed. She walked back to her filing cabinet and returned with yet another handout. "Here's an example from a late first century Christian writing."

> And then the child of the great God to man shall come incarnate, being fashioned like mortals on the earth... 888 will the name **reveal** to men who are giving up to unbelief.[6]

The professor looked up at Robert. "In this first century document, did the writer say he was *concealing* or *revealing* the person's identity with the number 888?"

Robert read the excerpt. "The number was used to *reveal* the person's identity."

"Precisely. In this Christian writing, the number of Jesus' name was used to *reveal* his identity, not to hide it. The writer of this document wanted unbelievers to know precisely whom he was talking about. That's why he wrote '888 will the name *reveal*'. And quite literally, given Jesus' fame in the first century, only a senseless or insane person in that culture would not know who this document was referring to. And that must be the same situation with the document you are referring to. If

---

6  *The Sibylline Oracles, Book I*, lines 393 - 399

the writer said 'anyone who has a mind' will know who a person is by their number, then you can be sure that the writer is referring to the number of a very prominent, very famous, person of that time. That's the meaning of the passage you are translating."

"Wow!" Robert exclaimed. "Thank you."

"You're very welcome. And I'm sure you'll find next week's class on this matter even more interesting and more enlightening. There was so much going on during this time regarding people's names and numbers — fascinating things."

Robert shook the professor's hand and headed to the door.

¤ ¤ ¤

When Robert returned to his dorm room, he was excited on one hand, yet upset on the other. He was excited that he might be able to find out who the Beast of Revelation was. Yet he was upset at the thought that Valerie's Bible had mistranslated the sentence. And he was also upset that her church didn't teach her how numbers were used to reveal people's identities in the first century. Instead, her church taught that numbers were used as complex riddles — the exact opposite of the way they were used in the first century.

Robert shook off his concern. "So the Book of Revelation wanted to reveal the identity of the Beast... not conceal it. And the number 666 must refer to an extremely prominent person — which is why Revelation's author wrote that only an idiot won't know who he was referring to. This means, the identity of the Beast can be solved with certainty. I *can* know who the Beast is."

Robert pondered all he had learned. Then he added the following entry to his journal:

CLUES TO THE BEAST OF REVELATION:

**The number of the beast's name is 666,** which means the sum of the symbols of his name is 666.

**Anybody with half a brain will know him by this number,** which means the beast was so popular that only a crazy person wouldn't recognize him by the number 666.

[End of Preview]

For more information visit:

www.TheUnhiddenBible.org

www.TubiPublishing.com

LaVergne, TN USA
02 January 2010
210702LV00005B/252/P